THE SPICE Girls

THE SPICE Girls

ANNA LOUISE GOLDEN

BALLANTINE BOOKS • NEW YORK

Copyright © 1997 by Anna Louise Golden

All rights reserved under International and Pan-American Copyright Conventions. Published in the United States by Ballantine Books, a division of Random House, Inc., New York, and simultaneously in Canada by Random House of Canada Limited, Toronto.

http://www.randomhouse.com

Library of Congress Catalog Card Number: 97-93476

ISBN: 345-41965-0

Text design by Michaelis/Carpelis Design Associates, Inc.
Cover design by Kristine V. Mills-Noble
Cover photo © D. Dyson/Camerapress

All photos by Mick Hutson, Brigitte Engl, Kieran Doherty, and Patrick Ford courtesty of Redferns

All photos by D. Dyson and Stewart Mark courtesy of Camerapress

All other photos courtesy of All Action

Manufactured in the United States of America

First Edition: April 1997

10 9 8 7

For
Jonathon and Judy
and Jayne,
With More Thanks Than You Know
You're All Such Good Mates, and I'm So Lucky

Contents

INTRODUCTION

*I*t seems as if the whole world has just been waiting for the Spice Girls. Everyone's mad for them. And well they might be. For far too long the boys have been ruling the charts, telling us exactly what they want, and having it all their way.

Now the tables have been turned. Five girls, sassy, outspoken, rude, sweet, a bit of everything and anything, just being themselves, have proved to be the biggest thing to hit the music business and the public in years. Top Band, Top Girls, Top Politics. "Wannabe," their first single and a song that is an amazingly catchy manifesto for Girl Power, has rocked to the top of the charts in thirty-seven countries, selling more than three million copies in the process, while the follow-ups, "Say You'll Be There," and "2 Become 1," both softer and sexier, have already been snapped up by over two million people around the globe, and still await release in America.

By itself, that would be amazing. But when you add the fact that their debut album, *Spice*, has gone platinum in seventeen countries, you can tell there's definitely something going on. Something major. It's beyond hot.

"Who's your favorite Spice Girl?" has become a question almost anyone, anywhere can understand—and probably answer. About the only way someone might not have heard of them is to be living as a hermit, away from newspapers, television, and radio. They've invaded the media—in Britain it's virtually impossible to open a daily paper or a magazine without reading something about them—and more or less effortlessly conquered it. Another picture, another quote, another bit of story from the past, another piece of advice for girls, the journalists are happy with any scrap they can get. The Spice Girls sell.

Four years ago they were nobodies, scuffling round the fringes of the entertainment industry, answering ads, attending auditions, taking whatever jobs they could find to keep body and soul together. Now they're parodied (on the British version of *Comic Relief*) by the likes of Jennifer (*Absolutely Fabulous*) Saunders and Dawn French. Peter O'Toole raises a laugh on England's *TFI Friday* TV show by sitting and reciting the lyrics to "Wannabe" with a straight face. The Spice Girls haven't just made it; these days they *are* it.

Of course, in Britain, pop trends appear and vanish as often as the tides. Being successful there is great, but let's face it, America remains the big one, and the hard nut to crack. In the nineties, only one British band has managed to make any real impression in the States—Oasis. According to all the critics, two battling brothers who can't afford enough eyebrows between them have been the biggest thing out of England since The Beatles.

Wrong.

The biggest thing out of England since The Beatles would be the Spice Girls. As it turns out, America hasn't even bothered to try to resist. It would have been futile, anyway. When you've got a song like "Wannabe" coming at you, sung by five girls with enough attitude to move mountains, you just roll over and accept fate. It's a foregone conclusion.

Of course, it didn't hurt that the song was quite deliberately aimed at the U.S.—note that Mel B raps "zee" instead of the British "zed" in the song. And that chunky mix of pop, R&B, hip-hop, and dance has proven to be just irresistible for everybody. Girls could identify with that you-want-me-get-with-my-friends-too message that Geri, Mel B, Mel C, Emma, and Victoria were putting across in the lyrics, and the boys could enjoy just watching them. Maybe they could even learn a thing or two about how to treat women these days. Only the surliest fan of alternative music and noise could have failed to have the cockles of his heart warmed.

And on these shores it's just starting. With only one single having charted in the *Billboard* Hot 100, going in at number eleven then leaping to number one—the first British female act ever to be number one—and an album very neatly poised in the top ten—it's simply going to get madder and madder. America is where the Girls will stage their premier performance with a live band, on the April 12 edition of *Saturday Night Live*.

The show might be well past its "sell by" date these days, but for one night at least, it'll be the liveliest thing on the planet. The country won't know what's hit it.

What it all means is that before you know it, there'll be Spice-type bands all over the place, as soon as the music business sees just how much money can be made. Maybe one or two will even have some small success sailing in the wake of the originals. But while they can be babes, no one else will ever manage to be the Superbabes.

When you get right down to it, does it really matter that someone else brought the Girls together? We're not talking about the Monkees here; this is the nineties, and these are five women with an agenda, not brainless smiles in matching clothes with a TV series to promote. By the time the public saw them for the first time, in June 1996, they were already raw, loud, blunt, bold, and in-yer-face—in other words, completely themselves. Definitely not mealymouthed little pop-star hopefuls, meek and mild, well mannered and eager to please the guys. Nor were they a bunch of bimbos, all bods and no brains. So how could this be the new manufactuing process for pop stars?

It wasn't, of course. Somewhere along the line the Girls had staged a coup and taken it all over for themselves. Yes, they were sexy, and totally up-front about it. What could be wrong with that? Who doesn't like to feel sexy? Sexy is good. But this bunch also came with a policy—Girl Power. While you could go out with them, have a drink and a good laugh, you'd better not mess around, mister, or you'd suddenly find yourself wishing you were miles away—in another galaxy, perhaps. The only way the green light came on was if they gave the signal. This was the new feminism, less serious, and maybe more powerful, than its hippie mother and academic big sister of the last few decades.

They weren't going to knock politely on the door and wait for it to be answered. They were going to kick it down and walk in as if they owned the place. And that's exactly what they did. In doing so, they just happened to speak for girls—and to boys—everywhere.

It certainly helped that they came armed with a bunch of great songs, catchy, soulful pieces just made for dancing (or slow dancing). But even there, the Girls weren't about to let anyone else put words in their mouths. They worked with professionals, the songwriting team of Stannard and Rowe and Absolute. But check out those credits: they've had a hand in the writing of every song they've sung. That's not manufactured. That's creation.

And that's Girl Power.

As Mel B defined it, "It's about equality and having fun and trying to rule your life."

Better make no mistake: for all the accusations of being pure plastic, of having a Svengali in the background, the Spice Girls very much rule their own lives. People might tell them where to be, and when, but after that no one's going to be able to tell them anything. They've made it because of who they are.

In Britain, they're the mirror of Every Girl who's out there slaving away in school or at a boring job, sick of being trodden on, waiting for the evening or the weekend to roll around so they can go out and have fun. They dress in the fashions and, in Mel C's case, the sportswear, that people buy every day from the High Street stores, the clothes Every Girl sees when she goes shopping at lunchtime, thinking of how she's going to spend her money.

If that's marketing, it's one of the coolest—and cheapest—tricks anyone's ever pulled. Emma noted that designer labels were exactly the same as those High Street clothes, "but a hundred times more expensive." When you're living on an allowance or you're a wage slave, who can afford to throw that type of money around? You've got better things to do.

It used to be that every female singer had to be permanently glamorous, to have a mystique that reeked of far too much spent on fashions and makeup. She had to be untouchable, well above the people who bought her records.

You'd better believe those days are over. The Spices pulled that notion down to earth with a bang. Not only did they dress like you, they talked like you. A mixture of accents, from the refined (Victoria) to the regional

(Mel B and her Yorkshire tones). They said in public the things you always wanted to say to everybody and could only dare when you were with your friends, the things all girls are thinking. In a world where sexual equality was supposed to be the rule, but all too often wasn't, the Spices ripped up the old book, then totally rewrote it. And everybody loves them for it.

They could—and have—talked about anything and everything. They'll tell you what they really, really want, and it's a lot more than just to zigzig ha. The lads do it, and since the Girls lowered the barriers, why shouldn't they, too? You want equal? Well, this is what it's all about. More than ten years have passed since Cyndi Lauper sang about girls just wanting to have fun, but it hasn't really been greatly in evidence. Well, somewhere along the line Emma, Mels B and C, Geri, and Victoria all took the idea to heart, because they *definitely* want to have fun. Go out, shop, have a drink, have a giggle, dance, meet guys—do anything they want to do. And talk about it all after.

Of course, for all that they make it seem easy, there's a lot of work that has gone into the entity known as the Spice Girls—a *lot* of work. Two years of practicing, learning, being taught how to sing and dance, of writing and recording songs. Like almost every overnight sensation, what you see is merely the tip of the iceberg. Even before they got together, when they each answered an advert placed in theatrical magazine *The Stage*, they'd all spent plenty of time in frustrated auditioning for singing, dancing, and acting roles. Geri had done some modeling, with her clothes on and off.

To be sure, the idea of putting together a girl group to raise hell on the charts was absolutely brilliant. The time was ripe. The nineties—in Britain, anyway—had been the decade of the boy band as pop wonders—the phenomenally successful Take That (whose fans even needed counseling when the group broke up), East 17, and, most recently, Boyzone. The only girl group to have made any sort of impact was Eternal, and they remained largely faceless, removed.

But whatever the impresario might have had in mind when he assembled and auditioned the girls, he was sadly mistaken. Several months later they'd rebelled against his control, signed up with a different manager, and the Girl Power Revolution was under way.

"She who dares wins" reads a slogan on the *Spice* album, a slight, sly corruption of the Special Air Service motto, but one that's perfectly appropriate. The Girls dared, risked it all, and they won. The future, at least in charts all over the world and in the press, is finally going to be very female. As *Melody Maker*, one of the leading British music weeklies noted: "High Street glamour, cartoon feminism and shouting. That's what we call a pop group."

Yes, their record company pushed them. But you don't achieve such international mega-success by hype alone. Certainly not thirty-seven countries in less than six months. There's got to be something behind it all. "Wannabe" was a perfect slice of pop, so catchy it should have been given a government warning about contagion. A great video, with Mel C's outrageous back flip—which she's also performed live on *Top of the Pops*—and chaos and fun exploding all over the place. It was obvious that no one could resist.

Especially when the Girls started popping up everywhere. By the time the record hit the top of the *Billboard* Hot 100, and the Spice Girls had cracked America wide open, just by walking on its soil, or so it seemed, they were an absolute, undeniable, unstoppable, certified phenomenon.

Girl Power ruled.

They'd achieved worldwide recognition, something no female British band—indeed, few artists of any nationality—had managed to do. They'd broken records and were creating new ones as fast as people could write them down. Their first three singles had all gone to number one at home—no female group had done that before. Indeed, it was a feat that only four bands had achieved—Gerry and the Pacemakers, Frankie Goes to Hollywood, the wonderfully named Jive Bunny and the Mastermixers, and Robson and Jerome. And in the U.S., entering the *Billboard* singles chart at number eleven, "Wannabe" tied the record for the highest-charting debut by an artist, set by Alanis Morissette with "Ironic."

If this was a pop fairy tale, then its ending was even better than living happily ever after.

For the first time, as *Select* editor John Davis observed, "you have a pop group occupying the teen market who seem to be the most approachable, human, flawed people imaginable. And they celebrate that they're not perfect. Which means, in a sense, that they can't fail."

Failure was never really in the cards, but could anyone have predicted the way Spicemania has erupted, that the whole world would take a collective sigh and embrace them?

Right now the future's so bright for the Spices that they must be pinching themselves on a regular basis

to be certain they aren't dreaming. The U.K. has a Spice Girls magazine. There are plans for Spice action figures (don't you dare call them dolls!)—maybe the first of their kind since G.I. Joe to be big sellers to boys—and the Girls have already signed to star in their first movie, which will evidently be a *Hard Day's Night*-style romp, the kind of vehicle that would be a perfect match for their irreverent personalities. John, Paul, George, and Ringo move over—the nineties have finally arrived and the Girls are here!

As if all that wasn't the icing on the cake, they've made an endorsement deal with Pepsi that will leave each Girl rolling in green to the very hummable tune of way over $1 million each. Sugar and spice and *lots* of things nice...

So plenty of people are putting their money where their mouths are and anticipating that the Girls are going to be around for quite some time. Fickle as fate might be, the next few years are quite assured for them.

Best of all, they've already become role models to a generation of girls. There are seven-year-olds showing attitude and spunk, learning that the word *female* doesn't have to equate with doormat, and that the lads and the lasses really can be equal. If those ideas stay with them, then Girl Power will be a lasting reality, and the Spices will have done a lot more than topping all the charts. They'll have totally changed the world.

As Geri said, "Okay, so a lot of people think [Girl Power is] just cheese, but if we can give anyone a bit of motivation, make any girl just sit up and go, 'I'm strong,' then that beats any number one or meeting any star."

They've got their heads screwed on right. They're having a great time these days, watching the world want them and laughing at it all, doing things "for the dare," like going up to London Suede singer Brett Anderson and announcing, "My mate Victoria fancies you." But behind it all, Girl Power is becoming insidious. Treat me badly and I'm just going to walk away, so you'd better watch your step, boy. It's the perfect antidote to the misogynistic ravings of all the rappers.

It would be easy for so much success so quickly to have gone to their heads, to leave them snobby and snooty. But that hasn't happened, and they're going to make sure it doesn't. They'll keep their feet very firmly planted on the ground.

"Being normal and being put into such a strange environment is the perfect combination," Mel B says. "I hope I can cling onto that normality—I'd be a horrible twat if I lost that."

And they'd lose all the girls who are looking up to them now. Girls who see themselves reflected in the Spices, who want to be as cheeky and brazen and outspoken, who've never seen anyone like them as stars before.

The world needs the Spice Girls. For the music and

the entertainment you'd be hard-pressed to find anyone better, as record sales show, but also for what they
have to say to the girls. And the way they keep the
boys firmly and funnily in their place, refusing to take
them seriously, showing just how juvenile and stupid
those male tactics can be.

Being who they are, saying what they do, they've
raised more than just eyebrows. Men don't know how
to handle women like this. They're frightened by
them, which makes them angry and defensive. Some
Southeast Asian countries went so far as to ban the
video for "Wannabe" simply because Mel B's nipples
were erect in a few shots. The Spices are trying, but it's
still a man's world...for now. But maybe not for much
longer, at least if the Girls have anything to do with it.

These days, Spice is the hottest commodity on the
planet. It's a spicy world. But when you've got it,
flaunt it, and that's exactly what they're doing. In
every way. They've worked hard to make it, and here's
the real Spice story....

THE SPICE Girls

CHAPTER • ONE

HERE WE GO

*T*he Spice Girls could never have been born in America. In a country that was founded by Puritans, the idea of having fun still seems to be a bit sinful, even more than two hundred years later. The nearest the United States has come politically to the Spices—the Riot Grrls—left quite a lot to be desired. The idea was good, girls in bands, playing guitars, making sure girls stood at the front at gigs, and woe betide any boy who manhandled them. The only problem was that they took it all so seriously. The music, and the girls themselves, were so dour and dire. It was as if they wanted to lose every trace of their sexuality, to forget that the human race was divided into male and female for a very good reason.

The Spices, on the other hand, celebrate the fact that they're women. Short skirts, revealing tops, flashes of Wonderbras; they play it to the hilt.

To understand how they could even come about, it's necessary to understand a little about Britain.

The early sixties there brought a real social revolution. Before that, you were either a kid or an adult. Virtually every school had a uniform, which you wore until you left, be it at fifteen, sixteen, or eighteen. In it, you were defined as a child. Once you were gone, you were an adult, working for a living, and you dressed the same way your parents did. Fashion, as such, might as well not have existed. To all intents and purposes, life was so drab that it might as well have been in black-and-white.

When all that changed, with The Beatles, Mary Quant, and a hundred others, it was as if someone had thrown a switch and put the color in everything. From being dull, boring, and quaint, suddenly London swung like a pendulum do. It wasn't just the capital of England anymore; to anyone under thirty it was the capital of the world. The miniskirt, the bands, the discotheques, the nightlife; in London *everything* was alive and buzzing. The Empire might have become something to read about in the history books, but suddenly there was a reason to celebrate Britain again. The Union Jack took on new life as a commercial symbol, on carrier bags, T-shirts, even underwear. England won the World Cup in 1966, another reason to be proud. They were the top dogs. There was full employment and economic boom. "You've never had it so good," as Prime Minister Harold Macmillan said, and it was quite true.

And it all happened to a sound track of pop music. Being geographically small, Great Britain—with its population of fifty-five million, around one fifth of the United States', the country would easily fit into Washington and Oregon, with plenty of room left over—had national radio courtesy of the BBC. In September 1967, wonderful Radio One was unveiled, all pop music, all the time. In homes and offices all across the nation, it played as background. Pop stars were feted in the daily newspapers. Young and old alike couldn't help but be familiar with what was going on. *Top of the Pops*, a very popular weekly television show, counted down the singles chart.

Pop culture ruled. Sometimes inane, sometimes ridiculous, it became woven into the fabric of everyday life until it seemed as if it had always been there.

Of course, a lot of things remained much the same as they had. The boys would go out together. Britain has always had a "lads'" culture, revolving around drinking, crude jokes, and soccer. On a Friday or a Saturday night, they'd start out in the pubs, have a few beers, and go to the Mecca or some other dance hall to try to pick up women.

The girls, too, had their routines. Going shopping on a Saturday at the big High Street stores, or the little boutiques that were springing up everywhere, then getting together in the evening to dance and talk and laugh. They could be every bit as crude as the men, but somehow hid it. When they danced, it was in groups, in circles, purses placed in the center of the ring for security.

Whether a boy or a girl, you went out with your mates. They were people you'd met at school, perhaps, that you'd grown up with. You knew them and they knew you. Still, plenty of things remained unspoken. However close you might be to someone, one thing you never discussed was your feelings or emotions. That was strictly off-limits. The stiff upper lip applied, as it always had.

It was still very much a man's world there. Some of the downmarket daily tabloids began running pictures of "Page Three Girls" (so called because they ran on page three, just inside the front cover), shots of topless models, and there was no shortage of girls eager to strip off and show their assets to a waiting nation. There'd always been a furtive market for "naughty vicar" stories in some of the Sunday papers, but now it was all up-front and out in the open. Sex and smut sold—at least it sold to men—and it was big business.

That was the world Victoria, Emma, Mels B and C, and Geri were born into. The first major change occurred when Britain elected a woman prime minister, Margaret Thatcher, whom Geri's often termed "the first Spice Girl."

In a way, that's exactly what she was. "The Iron Lady," as she was known, took office in a country that had spent much of the seventies sinking under the weight of its former glory. She was afraid of no one, a strong woman in a position of extreme power. While many would disagree with her politics (which were very similar to Ronald Reagan's), there could be no doubt she had a definite impact on the country. For those on top, the eighties were the wonder years. There was money to be made, and quite a few made it.

Toward the end of the decade, a whole new youth movement sprang into being. Inspired by the dance clubs young people had discovered on vacation in the popular Balearic Islands, off the coast of Spain, and fueled by the house music pounding out of Chicago, Acid House began, a wild time of raves in fields and abandoned warehouses.

It was out of this that the present dance culture was born. The sound of a thousand drum machines hammering away, turntables, synths, samplers all combining for the beat. The rave scene proper died, but in its place the dance scene took over the clubs, replacing the discos, and sometimes the bands. Gradually it invaded the English charts, moving from the crude early efforts to the extremely sophisticated as things became more commercialized. Like so many things before it, it trickled into popular culture, the backdrop for television shows and ads.

There was no way the Spices could have been unaware of it. It was everywhere. They were going out to dance to it themselves. It was a natural part of the language they heard as teenagers, clubbing on the weekends, just as their parents had gone dancing at the Mecca or the local discotheque.

In Britain, the nineties also saw the return of the "lad," shiny and polished and back in good graces—if he'd ever really left. In fact, he was almost lauded. Magazines like *Loaded* and *FHM* appeared. In a lot of ways, they were nothing more than *Playboy* or *Penthouse* with a fresher look and far fewer pictures. But there was more, an edge that has never existed in America (possibly apart from a few fraternity houses). These magazines said that it was perfectly okay to be rude, loud, and obnoxious, to think of women as "totty" (desirable), and try to persuade them to flash their boobs. It was a way of saying that men were still in control, and could get away with doing exactly what they liked. They could go out and get drunk, be as lewd as they desired, ugly, awful, anything, and the women of their fantasies should still be lining up to fulfill their every whim. Dreams? Of course, but a lot of men believed them.

The remaining factor was football, or soccer. At least, it's important to Mel C, an unrepentant fan of the Liverpool team, and to Mel B, who still supports Leeds United.

Not too long ago, soccer was the sport of the working classes. Men would go to the matches on Saturday afternoon, and boys wanted to grow up to play the game professionally. It was cheap entertainment, and great sport.

Somewhere along the line, that all changed, and soccer became a multibillion-dollar industry. The heroes of the British game are as well known there as a Michael Jordan or Ken Griffey, Jr., even if they're not paid quite as well. But with all the money, soccer changed its image. It became respectable, the game for everybody, not just the workingman. It reached into the grab bag and sprinkled on glamour.

Books like Nick Hornby's *Fever Pitch* contributed to the idea that soccer also had an intellectual side. The top teams, like Manchester United, Liverpool, and a few others, found fan bases well outside their hometowns. The game had gone mega.

All of these things together formed the weave of the Spices' lives, both growing up and as adults. This was their England, their time and place, the things that informed their lives every day, that they took in without even noticing.

Somewhere in there, too, was feminism. For any girl born since the 1960s, that, too, has been a part of life. Some of it we take for granted—women in politics and business, women being successful, enjoying careers and being fulfilled. But none of those things came easily. It's only in this century that women have been able to vote. And the concept of women as more than wives and mothers was a long, long, long time in becoming reality. Not until the seventies did that begin to really happen, and even then the woman was supposed to hold down a stressful, responsible position and be wife and mother as well, cooking, cleaning, doing everything she'd done before. To be Superwoman, in fact.

In theory, women and men are equal these days. Treated the same, paid the same, with all the same opportunities. At least, that's the theory. Reality, of course, is totally different. Eighty years after the suffragettes, the first campaigners for women's rights, were chaining themselves to railings and going on hunger strikes, it's still a man's world. It's the boys' club, all grown up and still trying to put up the signs saying NO GIRLS ALLOWED. To most men, women aren't just a different gender, they're a second-class race.

There are those who break down the barriers. Margaret Thatcher, that first Spice Girl, took the boys on at their own game, played harder than they ever could, and beat them. Whether you agreed with her policies or not, she was a tremendous role model. She'd made it to the top, and stayed there for eleven years—an incredible feat for anybody, especially a woman.

Feminism had always been about fighting for female rights, having a level playing field for everybody. But it seemed as if the women who'd been in all the battles had felt the need to downplay the fact that they were women. Makeup, good hair, nice clothes all went by the board. They were dour. All too often they were just frumpy. Maybe it was even understandable;

they needed to be accepted for who they were, not what they looked like. Besides, men had spent far too many years molding women into the images they created—large chest, long legs. They were still doing it.

Finally, women had had enough. They decided it was time to reclaim their sexuality. They could be tough and equal, and still manage to look attractive. In fact, taking their appearance into their own hands made it even more powerful. They could be exactly who and what they chose to be. And a lot of them chose to be sexy, to throw it back in the faces of the men who'd created it. That was probably the best statement of the lot. Women could have it all.

And so the stage was set for the Spice Girls.

CHAPTER · TWO

5 BECOME 1

*T*he real Spice Girls story doesn't start with the Girls themselves. By now it's common knowledge that they came together after answering an ad in the British magazine *The Stage* and passed the audition to become a new band.

That much is true. Well, more or less true. The ad was certainly placed, and Geri, Mel B, Mel C, and Victoria all passed the audition. A couple of them had even met briefly before. But there was a lot more involved in the process than that.

The story really begins with Bros, one of the major British boy bands of the eighties, which quickly faded into obscurity and bargain bins when the members went their separate ways.

Luke Goss, who, with brother Matt was the focal point of Bros, had been dating a girl called Nicky Herbert. Her father, Bob, was an accountant, a man who took something of a shine to the Goss boys, letting them rehearse in his summer house, building them up as what he called an "image group," and trying to interest record companies in their music.

It could have made Bob Herbert a rich man. Except for one thing—the contract he'd signed with Bros expired before they made it big. They signed with another manager, and Bob saw all his profits going to someone else.

That had been a few years before. Bros had their few moments in the sun, thought they could make it as individuals, and promptly vanished forever.

But, according to an exclusive story in the *Daily Mail*, written by Ceri Jackson and Annabel Cole, Bob's idea of making a showbiz killing wouldn't go away quite as easily. An idea was forming in his mind that could make all the money from Bros seem like a kid's allowance. He'd put together a girl group, call them Touch, make them seem real and strong, each one readily identifiable. And in partnership with his son, Chris, he set about turning his idea into reality.

The one thing the Herberts needed but didn't have was money. To be done right, this couldn't be a small operation. It would take time, and it would cost. So they called Chic Murphy, a man who'd worked with them on Bros. He was a Londoner, a man who'd been around the block a few times, having had a finger in any number of pies. At one point he'd managed seventies girl soul band The Three Degrees.

This new idea appealed to him. All the boy bands—young, innocent smiles, and expensive haircuts—had done very nicely on the British charts. The young girls

lapped it all up and bought their singles until someone newer and cuter came along. Then the bands
passed their "sell by" date and went back to school,
work, or whatever, and enjoyed the memories. But a
girl band...if it was done right, the possibilities were
almost infinite.

Murphy and the Herberts were agreed that they
wanted absolute control. They'd lost out on the big
payback with Bros, and they weren't about to let that
happen again. But Murphy was definitely in. He'd put
up the money for the whole operation.

It was interesting that they decided to advertise in
The Stage, a paper usually read by people looking for
stage and screen work. After all, they were putting
together a pop group, not a repertory company to perform Shakespeare. It would have been more obvious,
and probably more logical, to have placed ads in
Melody Maker or *New Musical Express*, the music weeklies. Bands had been doing that for decades with pretty
good success rates. And they were still doing it in
March 1994.

But Murphy and the Herberts knew exactly what
they were doing. They wanted girls who could act a
little, who could move and carry themselves. They
needed girls, as the ad said, who could sing and dance
(talents common to girls working in musicals) to put
together "an all-female act for a record deal."

If they were worried about the number of responses

they'd receive, their fears disappeared when they reached the rehearsal room they'd booked. Instead of sixty or seventy, there were over six hundred wannabe pop stars lined up and ready to strut their stuff.

Just listening to them all, hearing them talk, run through their party-piece numbers with piano accompaniment, then perform a tap or jazz dance, took up far too many hours. Most were awful. Of those who were good, plenty just didn't have the kind of personality or looks the men needed. Exactly what they wanted was still cloudy, but they'd know it when they saw it.

According to the Spices, Murphy and the Herberts had originally seen the band as one frontwoman and backup singers. A tried-and-true idea, it had worked for The Three Degrees and The Supremes, and there was absolutely no reason why it couldn't work again in the nineties. They'd be exactly the same as the boy bands, only female. In the months to come, it would be one of the major points of contention between the girls and their managers.

For now, though, there was still the hurdle of the audition to be overcome. A number of girls were called back and given the chance to perform at greater length. How did they project themselves? Did they have that mysterious and elusive star quality? Songs could be bought, routines could be choreographed, but a girl either had charisma, something that set her apart and focused eyes on her, or she didn't. You couldn't fake it, force it, or purchase it.

When everyone had been seen and heard, there were four girls who stood out. Geri Estelle Halliwell, a redhead, came across as loud, talkative, and saucy. Victoria Addams had a cool, haughty sophistication, the type that could easily keep men intrigued. Melanie Jayne Chisholm, from Liverpool, projected a down-to-earth normality, the approachable girl-next-door. Even though she wasn't the prettiest woman they'd seen, her nose ring lent her a hip air. Melanie Janine Brown, a Leeds lass, offered the great contrast, a contained wildness. Black, with a pierced tongue and a Chinese symbol tattooed on her stomach, she could easily be the jalapeño in the spices.

And then there was Michelle Stephenson.

Who?

Hers is one of a number of names that don't figure in the official Spice Girls history. But like Chic Murphy and Bob and Chris Herbert, she was there in the early days, selected from the audition to try to walk the road to stardom.

Michelle was a drama student. At heart she wanted to act, but this was an opportunity, and when you are struggling, you take any chance that presents itself. That was why they'd all shown up for the audition.

There have been a number of versions of the Spice Girls story. One states that Geri, Emma, Mel B, Mel C, and Victoria were all friends before they answered the ad, that they'd known each other from clubs and auditions, even that they'd come up with the idea of forming a band long before they met their manager.

It's lovely, it's romantic; in very many ways it's a shame that it's wrong. What is true is that each of the girls had spent plenty of time attending auditions, but with very little success. They'd all spent far more time working the dull jobs so many people end up in while seeking fame and fortune—waitressing, dancing, office work, anything that paid the bills.

Geri hadn't even made it to the audition. She'd desperately wanted to be there, but it conflicted with the offer of some paid modeling work, which she just couldn't afford to turn down. She'd called Chris before the tryouts and kept pestering him afterward. She wanted this so badly, and she was determined to do anything and everything to get it. Finally, after giving her a chance, the Herberts had to agree there was something about her, even if she was a little older than the other candidates. Geri, much to her joy, was in.

So, when they learned they'd passed the audition, maybe they all thought success was little more than a recording session away. It would have been quite understandable. And very hopeful.

This time Chic, Bob, and Chris were determined to do it *right*. Nothing would be rushed. The girls would be trained and groomed. They'd live together, work, eat, do everything together, and really get to know each other. They'd be individuals, but also they'd be a true band. There'd be singing lessons, dancing lessons, months and months of hard work ahead of them. And even then, there was no certainty it would work. The music business is littered with also-rans, people who've tried and failed to break through. Money and clever marketing would help, but the biggest factor was the most fickle of all—luck. They even gave the chosen girls two weeks to really think about the idea, whether they'd be willing to commit themselves to all the hard work necessary, living on a pittance, with no payoff definitely set for the future.

All five answered with an unqualified "yes."

With no guarantees, with not much of anything, really, the girls quickly settled down to their new routine. Chic rented a house for them on Boyn Hill Road, in Maidenhead, a sleepy little town about twenty miles outside London. The big city was far enough away to keep temptation at bay, but still accessible if they *really* wanted to make the trip.

For the most part, the girls were content to stay at home. Chic gave them each an allowance and made sure all the bills were paid, but they weren't exactly living in the lap of luxury. For girls who'd be earning millions of dollars in a few years, it was all pretty cheesy.

Pictures taken by Mel B's boyfriend of the time, Mark Brownsmith, show a run-down semidetached house (a duplex). Inside, the furniture was sparse, and what there was of it—a couch, a couple of chairs—was old and cheap, the gray carpet in the living room dirty and threadbare.

They were the kind of surroundings that would have caused a lot of girls to flee back home to the safety of their parents. But the Spices weren't a lot of girls. They were driven. Having passed the first hurdle, they could begin to taste fame, and they weren't going to let a few sticks of tattered furniture put them off their stride.

But all the determination in the world didn't stop them from being scared as they began their training at Trinity Studios, the place where the auditions had been held, and which Murphy now rented from owner Ian Lee for one hundred pounds a week. This was the real thing. People were risking a lot of money on the idea of them becoming stars; the pressure was beginning to build. Initially, they were teamed up with Irwin Keiles, a musician who'd helped the Herberts with Bros. A songwriter, it was his job to take the musical side of their career in hand, to mold their style and voices. And then there was record producer Michael Sparkes, who would later claim that "I made their sound, their management company built their image. They are totally, one hundred percent manufactured." Helping him was Pepi Lemer, a woman who'd worked extensively as a singer and voice coach.

"The first time I saw them," Pepi told the *Daily Mail*, "they'd had to learn this song that Irwin had written called 'Take Me Away.' I remember them being attractive in their different ways but terribly nervous. They were shaking and when they sang their voices were wobbling....My first impression was, 'My God, there's a lot of work to be done here.'"

Sparkes felt that only Mel C had any singing ability, although Mel B showed some improvement. And, he added, "I would say they were the worst-behaved band I have ever worked with."

Pepi was willing to spend the time with them, individually and as a group. At first, she thought they could manage with one long session each week, but that first performance convinced her that four hours, twice a week, was necessary if they were going to reach the standard Murphy and the Herberts wanted.

It was grueling, boring work, repeating notes, phrases, and harmonies over and over again. Every mistake had to be criticized and corrected. Lemer was a perfectionist, and the way the Girls sounded after her coaching was a reflection on her. She bullied, cajoled, and persuaded them to keep on going, telling them to sing it again.

At times, one or other of the girls would have enough, and tempers would begin to fray.

"One might have a headache," Lemer recalled, "the other would start crying, another would run out of the room, and the remainder would start arguing."

But every minute was necessary to their development. Professionalism was the key.

Still, there was also time for fun. The girls might have had their ups and downs, but they got along well together. They were always ready to have a laugh and cause a stir. They could be loud, have music playing late into the night. During the weekends, there would be parties for them to go to, to flirt and dance and relieve the tension of the week. And even when things weren't going so well, they all remained convinced that the big time was just around the corner.

Except for Michelle Stephenson. She worked and played every bit as hard as the others, but somehow it seemed as if she just wasn't quite cut out for the pop life. Frustrated and unhappy, she finally quit after the girls had been together a few months. Her heart wasn't in it. By the end, Mel B said, "She spent most of her time on the sun bed."

It was a blow, not only to the girls, but also to Murphy and the Herberts. They needed a replacement, and fast. Not just anyone, but a girl with talent, and the right kind of chemistry to blend in with the others. Pepi Lemer was given the job of finding her.

Luckily she knew someone who seemed as if she might be perfect. Abigail Kis had been one of Lemer's voice students when she taught at Kinsway College, in North London. She could sing, and with her dark-skinned Hungarian background, she looked good, and she performed well when the men auditioned her for the group. But it all fell apart when Chic took her on one side.

In his broad Cockney accent, he told her, "Look 'ere, gal, if you've got a boyfriend, you better give him the elbow, we want total commitment."

What he didn't realize—or perhaps he did, and was just testing her—was that Abigail's boyfriend of three and a half years had come down to the audition with her, and was standing in the same room. When they left, Abigail had a huge choice to make—to stay with her boyfriend, or plunge into being part of a group that was simply one of many with its eyes on the big time.

Two days later, Lemer called to offer her a place in Touch. But Kis wasn't certain if she wanted to take it. "It was a huge gamble," she told the *Daily Mail*. "I had a place at Middlesex University to do [a degree] in performing arts and I was not sure if I should give it up."

But there were other factors—the hard work involved in the training, living away from her parents, and being separated from her boyfriend when she "knew our relationship would suffer."

After taking the time to think things through Abigail called Lemer with her decision: She would keep the boyfriend and go on to college.

These days that's a decision she wishes she'd never made. Still only twenty, now living in London and working as an aerobics instructor, the boyfriend long since history, she told the *Daily Mail*, "Every time I see them I think, 'It could have been me.' I would have loved to have been that famous."

And indeed it could. But it wasn't (as an ironic postscript, Abigail would later meet her replacement, Emma, and say, "She was really nice"). Which meant that Lemer still had the vacancy to fill. After a lot of thought, she finally remembered a girl who'd studied with her in 1991 when she was teaching at a college in Barnet, North London, a pretty, pert little blonde named Emma Bunton who was taking her BTEC certificate. The problem was getting in touch with her. Lemer didn't have her address or phone number.

All Pepi could do was go to the college, search through the records, and follow up all manner of leads to track Emma down. It took a month, but finally she was able to come up with a phone number. Nervously she rang until a woman answered—Pauline Bunton, Emma's mum.

Lemer explained the situation, being very careful to emphasize that the chances of success were very small, even if Emma passed the audition. It was all a massive gamble.

When Emma, still living with her mother, arrived home from work, Pauline relayed the message and watched the excitement grow on her daughter's face. This was everything she'd dreamed about and hoped for. She called back, and Emma's audition was arranged. Lemer mailed a tape, asking Emma to learn one of the songs. A few days later everyone assembled in Irwin Keiles's Surrey studio to hear her. Emma's voice was impressive, but, Lemer told the *Daily Mail*, "Chic was a bit worried about her legs though, he thought they were too big. I said all young girls have weight problems and they didn't want some six foot tall, skinny blonde untouchable."

And with that, Emma was in, and the girls were finally assembled.

It had quickly become apparent that while all the girls were ambitious, it was Geri who was the hungriest for success. She was willing to put in the most work, and so it was ironic that in many ways she had the farthest to go. When Lemer first heard them all sing, none had been great. But she'd noted that Geri was "out of tune"—a report that Geri had seen, and which had greatly upset her for a while.

Now, seeing how it was all slowly coming together, the way she was improving, and sensing the potential of the girls, Geri just wanted to rehearse and rehearse. The professional in her needed to make it all work.

And that was why there was sometimes friction between her, Victoria, and Emma.

Emma had quickly fit into the group, giggling, laughing, and romping with the others. But while she enjoyed her freedom, and all that it offered, she also missed home, so every weekend she'd go back to visit her mother, whose house really wasn't that far away. And Victoria, whose parents also only lived a few miles away, did the same thing. To Geri, ready to work every single day, this was unprofessional. She was willing to make a total commitment—why weren't they?

But they managed to sort things out. Their singing

had improved beyond belief. It still needed work, but the thin, nervous, off-key voices Lemer had first heard had been replaced by something more tuneful and powerful.

As well as giving singing lessons, Lemer had somehow also taken on the role of social adviser. For all the jobs they'd had between them, the girls were still young and remarkably naive. If they were going to survive in the world of show business, a sea rife with sharks, there were plenty of skills they needed to acquire very quickly.

Each dressed in her own way—Mel C in soccer gear, sweats, and sports clothes; Mel B and Geri in short skirts and slightly trashy gear; Victoria in designer wear; and Emma in baby-doll dresses—and that was fine, but they needed to refine their looks and add some style. Lemer would give them items of clothing and teach them how to act in the social situations she hoped they'd eventually be in. She even tried to introduce them to food that was more than the basic burger and fries, a curry, or fish and chips.

"One evening I cooked them dinner," she recalled. "One of them poked at the smoked salmon and asked me why it wasn't cooked. They were incredibly naive and sweet."

But they still weren't quite ready for the big time. It was work, work, and more work. Anything and everything that could make them into stars.

Even after all these months, they still didn't have a

name that suited them. Touch had long since fallen by the wayside, and they'd become known as just the Girls. While that seemed more or less fine for now, something better was needed for when they were ready to catch the public's eye.

What they needed was a new name, which came to Geri while she was taking an aerobics class. The Girls had written a song called "Sugar'n'Spice," and suddenly it struck her that Spice would be ideal. It was short, it had a hot edge, exactly what they wanted, and it sounded good. Spice it was going to be.

Where the inspiration came from, she never said. But it might have happened locally, as their neighbors on Boyn Hill Road, an elderly couple named Brobyn, had a dog, a Lakeland terrier named...Spice.

"Occasionally the girls came over to ask my husband for help," Mabel Brobyn explained to the *Daily Mail*. "One time, they'd locked themselves out and he lent them a ladder. Spice was always around and we'd constantly be calling out his name. I'm sure that's where they got it."

However, there was a problem with Spice—someone was already using it, an American rapper. But the girls liked it; it just sounded *right* for them. With a little alteration, they could make it work. If they couldn't simply be Spice, then they'd be the Spice Girls.

They all loved it; it was perfect. Now they had an identity. Very soon they'd be ready to take on the world.

Date Due Receipt

Library name: ROMS_22

Author: Sebba, Anne.
Title: That woman : the life
of Wallis Simpson, Duchess
Item ID: 39082118515538
Date due: 9/23/2015,23:59

Author: Asfar, Dan, 1973-
Title: Ghost stories of
Michigan
Item ID: 39082125183601
Date due: 9/23/2015,23:59

Author: Golden, Anna
Louise.
Title: The Spice Girls
Item ID: 39082072492708
Date due: 9/23/2015,23:59

Fines may be charged
if items are not returned
by due date. Renew items
at: tlni.ent.sirsi.
net/client/roms

CHAPTER • THREE

WITH ALL THEIR HEARTS

With the name chosen, there was a definite change in feeling among the girls. After almost nine months of constant work—not to mention a fair amount of laughs in between—they felt they were ready to see what the Spice Girls were all about. They already had managers in Chic Murphy and Bob and Chris Herbert. The next step was to find an agent.

Obviously, no agent was about to sign them without having a chance to see them in action. The best way to do that was for the Spices to stage a showcase, to let people see exactly what they could do. They might have been put together from an ad and extensively coached, but really, what was the difference between that and band members finding each other from an ad, then spending months in a basement writing and rehearsing material?

The *idea* for the group had come from someone else, but at the end of the day, on stage or on record, it was all down to the Spices themselves. They looked like themselves, sang like themselves, and put their own, unique personalities across.

And by now those stage personalities were very strongly defined, as were the visual images each girl presented. Mel B, in spite of her stunning looks, had the wild hair and clothes to come across as "Scary Spice"—totally in yer face. Emma, with her young looks (she is the youngest in the band) and little-girl clothes, was now "Sweet Spice" or "Baby Spice." Victoria, with her upper-class looks and taste for expensive clothes, became "Posh Spice." Mel C, who thought of herself as "the plain one," and lived in sportswear and Liverpool soccer shirts, was "Sporty Spice," and Geri, the sultry redhead, was quickly hailed as "Ginger Spice" or "Sexy Spice."

Between them, they covered the whole gamut of female style. The Spice Girls were fully formed, and ready for the future.

For the showcase, Murphy and the Herberts rented Nomis Studios (owned by Simon Napier-Bell, an astute manager himself, who'd been involved behind the scenes with Wham! and George Michael; actually, a few unconfirmed rumors connected him to the Spices) in the Earl's Court area of London, and invited down representatives of the biggest agencies. The Spices were set to perform five songs, all written by Irwin Keiles, the man who'd worked on much of their musical training, and his collaborator, John Thirkell.

Everything had been meticulously planned.

But there was a big surprise waiting in the wings.

The Girls were about to take control of their own destiny.

They wrote a rap for one of the songs, and Keiles hated it. He offered to rewrite their words, but they refused. As of right then and there, the Girl Power revolution was under way.

If anyone imagined they'd been dealing with a group of bimbos, they were far wide of the mark. During all the time they'd spent at the house in Maidenhead, the two Mels, Geri, Victoria, and Emma came to realize they had plenty of ideas of their own. They weren't going to be one girl in front and the others in the background, the way Murphy and the Herberts had envisaged. They were going to be full, equal members of a group. The Spice Girls had five full members. And they had very well-defined ideas of what they wanted to say to everybody in their songs, ideas that went beyond the usual "I love you" of chart fodder. Maybe they didn't have the ability to write the music themselves (which has often been true of the world's greatest singers, all through history. People praise Sinatra and Streisand, but how many words or notes of their material did they write?), but they could write the lyrics. They were strong, ambitious young women, who felt that far too often girls were never given a chance, never heard, just written off as pretty decoration. They were very happy being female, and flaunting it, but they weren't going to be kept under the thumb of men. As far as they were concerned, the days when that could happen were ancient history.

"No one wants to be classed as a bimbo anymore," Mel C explained. "You can wear your Wonderbra, you can wear your mascara, but you've got a bit of intelligence....Don't rely on your sexuality, but don't be afraid of it."

That was an idea Emma took a little further.

"Just because you've got a short skirt on and a pair of [boobs], you can still say what you want to say. We're still very strong."

They were loud, proud, often lewd, and they weren't afraid of anybody or anything. If anything, their training had been too good. It had created a Girl Power monster that was turning on its creator.

However much they talked, though, they still had to prove themselves as singers. But they were going to do it on their own terms; that was what this revolution was all about. They needed to show they were more than a manufactured group, a figment of some man's imagination turned from fantasy into flesh. Keiles said they'd become "brazen," but if that was what it took to assert their independence, then that was what they'd do.

By all accounts, the showcase generated an incredible amount of interest. The agents had never seen anything like them before. Five girls who could sing— on key *and* in harmony now, thanks to the extraordinary tutoring of Pepi Lemer—who could fill a stage with personality, and entertain just by being themselves. They were sexy, savvy, smart, and they had style.

At that point it was pretty obvious that with the right push the Spice Girls were certain to be the next big thing in Britain. Bombarded by offers from agents, it only took a short time before the record companies heard about the Girls and began asking to hear tapes of them.

The spell had been cast.

Murphy and the Herberts were happy with all the attention that was being paid to the Spices within the business. But they were finding it harder and harder to get the Girls to go along with their plans. They had it all formulated, weighed, and sorted out. A whole future mapped out. Everyone would make money for a couple of years until the new stars came along and usurped the Girls' throne, and then it would all be over.

None of which was part of the Girls' vision for the group. Sure, they wanted the money, the fame, fortune, and adulation—who wouldn't, given the opportunity?—but they were becoming more and more convinced that their way was the right way. They were young; they could speak more directly to girls and boys—especially girls—than any professional lyricist just looking for a clever rhyme. And their biggest asset, apart from their looks, was the fact that they could be themselves.

It was a situation with no easy solution. There was no doubt that the girls were grateful to Chic, Bob, and Chris for bringing them together, but the fact was that they'd outgrown everything the men had had in mind for them. They'd moved past all that.

When it came down to it, the only answer that would work was for them to find new management. But that posed problems, too. A lot of time and money had been invested in the Spices, money neither Murphy nor the Herberts wanted to lose. And that was certainly fair enough.

There was never a thought of the Girls buying their own contract. For a start, the only money they had came from Murphy. And they were smart enough to know that they needed a manager with experience and connections if they were really going to make it. But it had to be someone they could work with, someone who'd accept what the Spice Girls were.

So Murphy cast around for a person who might be interested, working quickly. Interest in the Spices was still rising; they were being inundated with offers from agents and record labels who could sense the potential there. It didn't take him long to come up with a suitable candidate.

Simon Fuller had been around the music business for quite a while. His company, 19 Management, had handled the careers of a number of artists, including Annie Lennox, once part of Eurythmics, and a strong woman who wasn't about to let herself be dictated to by anybody. His success rate was good, and he wanted to manage the Girls.

The deal was made quite amicably. Murphy and the Herberts walked away with a profit (although exactly how much has been kept a deep secret), Fuller knew the future was going to be golden, and the Spices were more than happy with their new manager. But one person they couldn't forget was Pepi Lemer, who'd given them so much of her time, energy, and expertise. After signing with Fuller, they sent her a card that read, "Thank you for everything, we could not have done it without you," hardly the gesture of superstar wannabes who were just using people to claw their way to the top, but rather the action of real, genuine girls with hearts and feelings.

Still, it had been time to move on, and signing with Fuller definitely seemed like the right move.

"Simon was really cool," said Mel B. "We had so many managers saying, 'Dress like this, sing that song, I can make you big stars.' Simon was really laid-back and understood that we wanted a say in how our careers would go."

Just how much of a say in those careers was increasing all the time. They were eager to be involved in the writing of the songs they were going to sing. They had ideas and demanded to be heard.

And they would be.

Chapter · Four

Who Do You Think You Are?

Of course, very little of that figured in the "real" story, which read more like a fairy tale with a happy ending than anything approaching reality. It took months of digging before the English *Daily Mail* revealed the truth in February 1997—and the *Mail* was only one of a number of newspapers that had been digging. The Fleet Street tabloids have a reputation for bulldog tenacity when it comes to getting to the bottom of stories, especially if there's anything sensational to be found down there, but most reporters simply couldn't unearth any information. Jane Atkinson, a writer for the *Sun*, Britain's biggest-selling tabloid daily, could only speculate that the Spices had argued with their management and gone elsewhere.

"Obviously," she concluded, "this is a situation where he might say, 'I want a cut, 'cause I made you who you are.'"

Certainly the Girls themselves didn't spill the beans. In interviews they hedged around the issue and, when prodded, claimed they couldn't give the names of their original managers "for legal reasons...."

All manner of allegations were soon flying about. Some journalists in England claimed that the group was scared to disclose the truth because of possible intimidation by Virgin Records, the Spice Girls' label—although intimidation of what nature, no one seemed willing to say. It was all incredibly vague.

So when the truth finally did come out into the open, even if a few people still whisper darkly that there are more revelations to follow, the biggest question seemed to be, "So what?" Truth might have been a little stranger, and certainly more convoluted, than fiction, but there was really nothing in there to harm the Spices. Quite the opposite. They still came across as strong young women who'd learned and grown a great deal in a very short time. Their image and message was still very positive. There was absolutely nothing wrong in coming together after answering an ad. Whatever kind of ideas the Herberts might have had, they'd been supplanted by something more powerful. The Spices were very far from being a nineties, female version of The Monkees. They went way past cute and cuddly. They were outrageous. They were *real*.

And this made it all the more baffling that such a false story had to be spun in the first place. Sure, it was more romantic to say they'd all been friends for a few years, that they'd met at auditions and clubbing around London, but in the end, who really cared about *how* they'd formed? It was the music that mattered, and the attitude, and they had plenty of both to spare. So why all the mystery and the secrecy? Then there was speculation among the press that Virgin had been doing quite a bit of cosmetic work on the Girls' image, including slicing a few years off everyone's age, and based on the first pieces of publicity, that really did seem to be the case, although why the company found it necessary to do this was never said.

According to the legend that the press agents put out when the Spices released "Wannabe," the formation of the band seemed almost inevitable. It was sheer coincidence that five of the girls who answered the ad in *The Stage* and who were then picked for the group (initially named Touch) already happened to know each other. Mel B and Mel C had supposedly been in the same dance company at one point—and had possibly even been roommates. Geri and Victoria had met while auditioning for parts in the *Tank Girl* movie (or, according to yet another story, while in line to actually see the movie). Victoria and Emma had been in a musical together when they were kids (one source even had them attending the same school!).

Once they'd decided they could work together as a band, they spent a few months crammed into a flat in the London suburbs, getting to know each other properly, working on their singing and dance routines, and starting to write songs together.

However, their manager had other ideas about how the Girls should be presented, and the five, now united, decided enough was enough. They were going to do it their way, and no one else's. They bought their way out of their contract and took charge of their own lives.

Needing more room to work and rehearse, the story continued, the Girls moved to a three-bedroom house in Maidstone, away from London in the Kent countryside, where they concentrated on their writing, gradually putting together a demo tape of material. Now they needed an agent, a publisher, and a manager.

To help with the first, the Girls all talked to their parents, who banded together and put up the money so they could rent Nomis Studios for a showcase, which proved to be very successful.

But they were still without a good manager, and kept circulating their tape around management companies, trying to find the perfect person to represent them.

It took a little while, but they finally located him in Simon Fuller, the man who managed Annie Lennox. They agreed to work with him on getting a record contract, but they wanted to approach it in a slightly different way from most bands....

The usual method was to send a tape to the artist and repertoire department, known simply as A&R, and hope someone listened to it, and liked it enough to want to hear more. The Spice Girls weren't about to settle for that, and let some faceless man be in control of their future.

They began invading record-company offices, performing their songs a cappella for the executives, and winning everyone over with their material, their act, and their feisty personalities. After they'd done a few of these, plenty of labels began contacting Fuller, all desperate to sign the Spices.

One thing that's beyond any doubt is that the contract was signed with Virgin, although the amount of the advance the Girls received has varied from 500,000 pounds sterling to two million pounds—quite a wide range.

For the signing, supposedly, they all arrived carrying inflatable dolls, which were thrown into the River Thames in a fit of exuberance.

That was the legend, and it did resemble reality here and there. Without a doubt it made people think of the Spices as a "real" group, which was obviously its original intention, although in all honesty they were never anything less, and it portrayed them as strong women, which also happened to be perfectly true.

So why the need to drape everything in a mass of hype?

Part of the answer lay in the way the Girls were being marketed, of course. It was one way to make them seem fresh and new, to help them stand out. Tales like this were the kind of thing the press lapped up. They would generate interviews, pictures, all kinds of publicity. And for a group hoping to make it big in pop music, publicity was necessary. "Wannabe" had to explode, and the Girls needed to quickly become familiar faces if they were going to be more than one-hit wonders.

In many ways, it was harder for them to burst onto the British pop scene than it had been for all the boy bands. The boys had a built-in audience of girls always on the lookout for new young hunks. Who could the Spices look to for their fan base?

Boys didn't buy as many records as girls; at least, they didn't buy as many singles. The band wasn't aiming at an adult audience, although they were sure to acquire some sort of male following, even if it was only for the way they looked.

So what they needed was publicity. And that was why the good story helped. Publicity made them an item, and once "Wannabe" had taken off, *Spice Girls* more or less became part of the national language in Britain.

In the beginning, though, no one anticipated that they'd have much to say. Pop stars, after all, weren't exactly known for the breadth of their conversation or the depth of their intellects. The big surprise came when the Girls began talking about Girl Power. It was a daring move for them to make, really, and certainly countered all the lightweight fluff pieces that were starting to be written about them.

Certainly, they were laying it all on the line. Their

lyrics, everything they said and did, were a reflection of what they believed. And in talking this way, they could easily have turned off a potential audience—did most people want to have to deal with strong women?

Men might have been a little scared, but soon began to realize that behind the Spices' up-front attitude and in-yer-face tactics, they were really five very nice, very normal girls. They just happened to have some different ideas about relations between the sexes. They weren't going to let themselves be doormats.

But while the men were wondering what was going on, the girls understood. At last, after years and years, someone was speaking directly to them. Someone was putting all their thoughts and frustrations into words and singing them to a hummable tune. For girls, the stance of the Spices was perfect. No-nonsense, even slightly abrasive, they stood up for themselves to loudly put their message across. And it was received and understood. Let the guys like the Spice Girls for the tunes and the way they looked. The girls wanted to buy the records because of the words.

Having *any* kind of depth made the Girls a rarity in the world of pop acts. The Spices might not have taken themselves totally seriously (and still don't), but the lyrics, well, that was a different matter altogether. Those, and the Girl Power position, put them in a different league from any other act aimed at the charts. They had the kind of credibility usually reserved for indie, alternative bands, groups who claimed to have some deep and life-changing message to put across.

The Spices just happened to be a lot more fun.

Both Geri and Emma have observed that the group works on two levels, and there's never been anything wrong with that. Catch 'em with the big pop hook, then educate 'em with the message. It's a great way to let things sink in. After all, pop and politics have never mixed that well. Who needs to be taught when they're trying to enjoy themselves?

But the Spicy method was easy on the eyes and ears for everybody. Very carefully constructed, and very clever.

Still, to put it all down to some brilliant marketing strategy would take a lot of credit away from the Girls themselves. The "official" story might not always have been in very complete agreement with reality, but initially it did serve its purpose—people looked at the Spices as a real band, not some manufactured confection. And the public does prefer the idea of a "band" and its sense of spontaneity, as if one was the right way, and the other completely wrong. A strange thought, really: which would you rather have—a car someone had put together at home, bashing the parts to make them fit, or one that had been manufactured? Only in music is *manufactured* a dirty word.

And no one could have reckoned with the Girls being who they were. From the first time they sat down to an interview, it was obvious that they weren't anybody's mouthpieces. They might, at first, have spouted the party line concocted by the publicists, but give them a moment to free themselves from the leash and they became the real thing—mad, bad, and possibly dangerous to know—in the very best way. They were outrageous, they really didn't seem to care what they said and did.

In other words, they were brilliant copy.

With all the parts put together perfectly, they had so much going for them that it was impossible to believe they wouldn't go straight to the top.

"Officially," it's always been said that the Girls spent a long time writing material for their album and singles with other artists (given the credits on the CD, it would have been impossible to claim otherwise), but no real kudos have ever been given to people like Pepi Lemer who helped mold five girls randomly thrown together into a very professional outfit. And that's a pity. Professional singers of all kinds, from opera stars and balladeers to pop heroes, regularly work with vocal coaches. They all have to keep their voices in top shape. There's certainly no shame in using one.

Still, revising history has always been part of the public-relations game. However it happened, it had absolutely no negative effect on the Girls' success in the long run; it may even have contributed to it. The newspapers didn't for one minute believe the "real" story they were being handed—they knew how the game was played—and went digging for the truth. It took them a long time, but eventually they discovered it, along with a number of other things about the Spices that simply helped to keep them on the front pages for months.

The truth will out. But by the time it became known, no one thought any less of the Spice Girls. By then, it really didn't matter anymore. They were mega all over the globe, and in England they'd become virtually a national institution. It had all gone way beyond anyone's wildest dreams.

Yet, in reality, there was still a distance to go. The fantasy the publicists created was fine; back in the real world, there was still plenty of work to be done....

CHAPTER·FIVE

BACK TO REALITY

For all the talk about the way the Spice Girls were created by some Svengali, that obviously wasn't the case. While a number of people had a hand in putting them together and setting them on the right road, everyone in the music business needs contacts, friends, and mentors. And while Murphy had deep enough pockets to give the Girls time to find themselves, when he tried to mold them into something they weren't, they had the integrity to say no. This wasn't stardom at any price; this was strictly on their own terms.

But people believe what they want to believe. If it's sensational, they'll read it. And a lot of people, all around the world, have been reading so much about the Spice Girls and the way they were "manufactured" that it's become an accepted fact.

"We could sit here all day and scream that we are not manufactured, we write our own music, we dress how we want to dress, and we're best mates," Emma complained in *Entertainment Weekly*, "but the fact is, it's not our problem if people want to think [otherwise]."

Still, people are always eager to think the worst of pop music. There's a feeling that you have to be "alternative" to have any kind of credibility, and that pop is nothing more than disposable rubbish, that it can't contain any kind of geniune message, simply because you can dance to it or hum and sing along with the words. It's a very narrow-minded attitude, very snobbish. A long time ago Elvis was a pop singer, and he revolutionized music. The Beatles were a pop group, and they managed to change the world. Madonna's never been anything other than pop, and she influenced an entire generation.

The Spices were a pop band, and proud of it. Now all they needed was a record deal.

That was Fuller's job. There was already plenty of interest in the Girls. Almost every major company wanted their signatures on a contract. Even before they'd set foot in a real recording studio, the Spices were a very big deal.

In May 1995, when Fuller and the Girls finally decided to accept the offer of a reported 500,000 pounds sterling (around $750,000) from Virgin Records—a label not known for putting out pure pop music—they did it in the style that would soon become the Spicy trademark. They went down to see deputy managing director Ashley Newton (the man who would oversee their records and publicity), burst into his office, and just went wild. The Girls were all talking at once, singing a cappella—there had already been one or two accusations in the business that they couldn't sing; after so many sessions with Pepi Lemer, they definitely had something to prove—just being themselves, being funny. Not surprisingly, Newton was overwhelmed. He called in managing director Paul Conroy and deputy managing director Ray Cooper to witness the event.

And why would such a label, whose background was in rock (Iggy Pop, the Sex Pistols, and so many others), even want the Spices? According to Newton, it was simple: "They've got credibility and are a convincing pop act. Their music is bright, sexy, and they have a spirit of camaraderie."

That was what the Girls could offer Virgin. But what could the label offer them? Quite simply, a lot of freedom to be themselves. While the other companies wanted to mold them, have them sing, act, and dance alike, Virgin immediately liked what they saw. They knew that work was needed before they made their debut, but realized that all the basics were already in place. If it wasn't broke, they weren't going to fix it. The idea of the Girls being different—real individuals, and real people, rather than untouchable pop stars— was appealing.

The thing that really clinched the deal, though, was the song "Something Kinda Funny." It was the first thing the Spices had worked on while trying out new writing partners, in this case the team of Andy Watkins and Paul Wilson (a/k/a Absolute), and

Newton heard a tape of it. As someone who'd grown up on and still loved soul music, he was immediately hooked by the vibe and the sound. As he put it, "I couldn't resist."

Geri told *DJ Times* that, "Something Kinda Funny" was "a reflection of what was going on with us at the time....Remember to enjoy the adventure, the journey—it's just as important as when you arrive."

With management and a label in place, it was time to get down to some serious songwriting and recording. And that meant finding some professionals to help them turn what they did into tuneful magic in the studio.

Apart from Absolute, they found very sympathetic ears in Richard Stannard and Matt Rowe, who worked under the name Biff n' Memphis.

"We didn't want a run-of-the-mill producer," Geri said in *DJ Times*. "We worked with soul boys and remixers who were undiscovered and open to letting us lean over their shoulder and say, 'Would you turn up that bass line,' or 'Would you put a little more EQ [equalization] on that vocal.'"

As far as the actual writing went, Geri insisted that, "The top line melodies come from us, and we work with technicians who translate what we're doing."

Given that only two of the Girls play instruments— Geri the guitar "very badly," and Victoria "very basic keyboard"—there was no doubt that they needed help, and it's something they've never tried to hide or deny. Matt Rowe quite openly admitted that, "Clearly, they had no formal writing skill."

Still, said Geri, "We all know what we want them to end up sounding like."

So, far from being anything artificial, the Girls kept input and control through the entire process.

"I think their appeal is such that people initially think, 'Hang on, this is a manufactured band,'" Rowe's partner, Richard Stannard, observed. "But everything was there, right from the beginning—the attitude, the philosophy, the 'Girl Power' thing....They had all the ideas for the songs, and we'd sort of piece them together, like a jigsaw puzzle."

It wasn't a quick or easy procedure. The Girls might have been brimming over with ideas, but setting them to music, and then arranging them, took many months. After they'd composed a catalog of thirty songs, the Spices sat down with their various producers and writing partners to begin a weeding-out process. Soon they'd have to go into the studio, and they wanted the very best, the strongest material for their debut album. When the songs had been chosen, the arrangements had to be refined, everything pushed to make it as good as it could possibly be. After all the work they'd put in—well over a year already—there was no point in producing anything less than perfect. Finally they narrowed it down to fourteen songs, including "Something Kinda Funny," which had become something of a good-luck charm for them.

The lyrics were revised again and again, polished and honed by the Girls until they said *exactly* what they wanted. Meanwhile the musical teams of Absolute and Biff n' Memphis were busy in their studios, programming drum tracks and loops, recording keyboards and backing tracks. The work was carried out at Olympic, a large old studio in central London that has seen endless bands pass through its doors over the years, and at the Strongroom, a newer facility in Shoreditch, East London. It looks run-down on the outside, hidden away in a cobblestone yard behind tall old gates and a stone archway on a slightly seedy street, but inside it's state-of-the-art, used by many up-and-coming bands, particularly those who rely on synths and drum machines rather than the standard guitars, basses, and kits. Most importantly, both studios had reputations as good places to record vocals.

Apart from the teams of Stannard and Rowe and Watkins and Wilson, the Girls also collaborated with Kennedy and Baylis on "Love Thing" and Kennedy alone on "Say You'll Be There," both of which had made the final cut for the album.

Once all the backing tracks were completed, it was time for the Girls to take the plunge, to remember all Pepi Lemer had taught them, and everything they'd since worked out for themselves. This was where the Spice adventure *really* began.

For all that the pressure was on, and that studio

time was expensive, the Girls had fun recording. Yes, it was serious business, requiring long, often tedious hours of work, but they all felt a great sense of joy as they stepped into the vocal booths, put on the headphones, and listened to the tracks. Even when day extended into night, and take after take of the same line or verse was required, they were together to make each other laugh, flirt with the engineers, have a tea or coffee and a burger, and know that something magical was happening.

Stannard and Rowe and the Absolute boys were all studio professionals, well versed in all the digital tools available, and also experienced in coaxing the best performances from singers and musicians. That was what they were being paid to do. But by now the Spice girls were professionals, too. All the months of practicing, working together, harmonizing, and freestyling off each other were finally paying off. This was for real. They didn't just go in to rock the house; they were aiming to rock the world.

By the end of 1995, the recording was complete, the tracks "in the can." The songs had been mixed—the various vocal and instrumental tracks played with and then joined and layered into the final sound chosen for the record—at a number of studios around London, Olympic, Larrabee North, and Townhouse, where the Girls had made sure their input was heard.

Even surrounded by real pros, they weren't going to sit in the background like bimbos and accept anything that was given to them. For everyone else involved, this was a job. To the Spices, this was *life*, and quite rightly they weren't going to blindly hand over control of it to someone else.

Finally it was time to deliver the master tapes to Virgin Records. The label had been keeping a close eye on the recording sessions. That was only natural. They were banking, quite literally, on the Girls being huge in Britain, and hopefully in a number of other countries. But shrewd as they were, there was no way they could have foreseen, or even engineered, the way Spicemania would take over the globe. No one knew it yet, but they didn't have simply an all-female pop group on their hands. They had an international phenomenon.

Even the Spices themselves, confident as they were—and had to be—about eventual success, had no idea that they'd soon be taking the world by storm.

Meanwhile Britain was sleeping its way through another gray winter. Mel C's beloved Liverpool team was doing well, but not well enough. Mel B's team, Leeds United, had signed a Ghanaian player, Tony Yeboah, who was setting the Premier League alight with some scintillating goals, but Leeds wouldn't capture the top spot, either.

On the charts, 1996 began with Babylon Zoo's "Spaceman" at number one, the fastest-selling single in British history, a mixture of glam, spacey sounds, and a techno beat that had come to everyone's attention when it was used as the music for a jeans ad. Take That, the boy-band phenomenon of the decade, had split up (although they had enjoyed a "posthumous" hit with a cover of Cat Stevens's "Father and Son"), leaving many girls in mourning for their idols even as the former members of the group began to issue solo records. East 17, who'd been doing very nicely, thank you, seemed poised to take their places in female hearts, but their grungy, outdated look wasn't quite the thing (and by the time the year was over, they'd have sacked one member for advocating the use of ecstasy, a drug that had killed several teenagers at raves and clubs). Instead, it was Boyzone who slipped into the void left by Take That's demise. They were bland and completely inoffensive. Definitely cute, but ultimately without any real personality, and quite disposable. Still, '96 looked as if it might be their year, as they quickly chalked up a top hit with a version of the old Bee Gees song "Words." Everyone was predicting major things, and they were starting to happen. But Boyzone, and everyone else, would only have half the year to revel in their glory. By July, the Spice Girls would eclipse everything else. And they'd do it at a speed that would seem to be rapidly approaching that of light.

Since the completion of recording, the Girls had hardly been idle. The studio was merely the start of things. Now there was choreography to learn, both for their upcoming videos and for performances, yet more rehearsals of the songs—once again for performances—and finally, the hardest task of all, they had to go shopping for new clothes. With plenty of time in the public eye ahead of them, each of them needed a new wardrobe.

In April 1996, the Girls began to understand the whole business process, as Virgin introduced them to the press. At that time very few people were interested (three months later they were all clamoring for interviews). "Wannabe" had been selected as the first single, and the video had been filmed, but the Spices remained an unknown quantity, one that could just as easily sink as swim. Quite understandably, the members of the press decided to hedge their bets and wait.

Music Week was interested enough to talk to them, however, to try to get a sense of what the Spice Girls might be about. The Girl Power agenda, it seemed, had to remain on the back burner for the moment; only when they really had people listening could they start on that—and have people hear what they were saying. For the moment they were another bunch of young hopefuls, pretty girls with a good song who might or might not go places.

Naturally, they stuck to the story that had been decided upon as the "official" line. Yet once they got started, they still managed to speak their own minds.

Geri's feeling was that the Spices wanted to return some glamor to pop music, "like Madonna had when we were growing up. Pop is about fantasy and escapism, but there's so much bull—— around at the moment. We want to be relevant to girls our age."

And Mel B scored a good comparison when she brought up Neneh Cherry, the woman who had an American hit in the late eighties with a dance/funk/rap song called "Buffalo Stance."

"She was a ballsy, sexy woman from out of nowhere with a completely new attitude."

You could find definite comparisons between "Buffalo Stance" and "Wannabe." Both were British, catchy as a cold, and crossed the lines that usually separated funk and pop. Both contained raps. And both advocated women being strong. There was absolutely nothing wrong in being part of that tradition. Except that after "Buffalo Stance" Cherry's hits more or less dried up, even if her songwriting career flourished.

Music Week felt that the Girls had a very bright future, one that could topple the status of bands like Oasis, saying, "The boys with guitars had better prepare for battle."

Now all they had to do was wait for the release of "Wannabe" on June 24.

For the video of the song, completed earlier in the year, the Spices had taken over a London club for a day. Without its normal crowd of people, the place seemed large and remarkably cold, a fact that was reflected in all the goose bumps the Girls had. It was quite notable that the directors had been chosen not for their experience with music videos, but because of a very successful television ad in Britain for a brand of jeans named Diesel. But that was what this video was, essentially—an ad for the Spices, a calling card to let people know they were here, and that they meant business.

It was a long, tiring experience for everyone concerned, as Emma remembered. "We recorded it about ten or fifteen times," she said, "so I think we all lost quite a bit of weight that day."

And given how athletic the clip was, that might not have been an exaggeration. The highlight, of course, was Mel C's athletic back flip, but she wasn't the only one in motion. Mel B, Emma, Geri, and Victoria were all hyperkinetic in the energetic video.

Maybe that was all for the best, given that Mel C's main memory of the day was of "how cold it was. It was really cold and we had them little tops on!" she recalled, adding a little suggestively, "Can't you tell?"

People could tell, but they didn't seem to mind one bit.

The first time the public heard the Spice Girls was on a cable television show called *The Box*, which showed the "Wannabe" video a few weeks prior to its release. It was a test run, really, to gauge public reaction. And that reaction was overwhelming. In the history of the show, no unknown group had ever generated such feedback. The switchboards were jammed. Who were they? What was the song? When was it coming out?

The next week, "Wannabe" was featured again, and

there was the teasing promise of something very special for the following show. It proved to be a specially filmed video clip by the Spices, an introduction to them and their world. The rap on "Wannabe" had given very brief hints about the personalities of the Girls. This went a little deeper.

The people in the U.K. who had cable TV now knew all about them, but what about the rest of the country? It was time for the Girls to take care of that, too, traveling from radio station to radio station all around Britain, singing live on the air, clowning, just being themselves, as wild as they wanted. And once they followed that with a series of broadcasts on Radio One from various coastal resorts, the name of the Spice Girls was becoming very familiar indeed.

The Spice Girls had landed, and Britain didn't know what had hit it.

As soon as "Wannabe" appeared in the stores, it began to sell by the cartload. The Spices were hot. You could hardly turn the radio on without hearing the song; it was always blaring out from somewhere. The video jumped straight into heavy rotation on MTV. All over the country, people at school, in pubs, cafés, even at home, were ready to tell you what they really, really wanted.

It was a song so full of hooks that it simply couldn't fail to catch attention. From the moment it began, with feet clattering down a hallway and a laugh, it leaped straight into your face, with Mel B and Geri trading off on the introduction over a simple, catchy bass line before moving smoothly into an R&B verse. That would probably have been more than enough to send it rocketing up the charts, but there was plenty more going on. If you stopped to really listen to the words, you discovered that they were more than the usual pop garbage. This was about women standing up for themselves, saying that they weren't going to tolerate being treated like dirt, walked on like a rug. These were girls with friends, with pride, who realized that some things were more important than just having a boyfriend. If you wanted one of these girls, you'd better get along with her friends and win her approval. And you'd for sure better treat her right, or she was gone. No questions, no second chances.

That was a pretty powerful message for the Top 40, and a very positive one.

And just *what* was that "zigzig ha," anyway? (A hint: It wasn't, as one American journalist seemed to think, slang for a cigar....)

The single's B-side was a much frothier confection called "Bumper to Bumper," which wouldn't even make it onto the Spices' eventual album. It was probably just as well that the song was more lightweight—"Wannabe" didn't need any competition. Having said that, you have to admit that the song has plenty of good points, a strong bass line and beat, and a slyly suggestive lyrical metaphor about a traffic jam and gridlock (which could easily have been inspired by Grace Jones's hit "Pull Up to the Bumper"). There was a New Jill Swing rhythm, and an R&B groove, sensuous and sexy, while the synthesizers took their deep sliding cues from old hits by the Gap band, plunging all the way to the subbasement and giving the woofers a full workout. Vocally, as with everything else, all the Girls were featured. As they'd insisted all along, this was a *band*; there would never be one up front and the rest in the shadows. And the song let people know that the Spices were down with the dance clubs, and that they had an impressively wide musical range of interests.

In its first week, "Wannabe" vaulted straight to number three on the charts, and the Spices were invited to appear on *Top of the Pops*, British television's long-running weekly chart show. They didn't send the video, they came in person—Geri, Victoria, Mel C, Mel B, and Emma crammed onto a small stage in the studio, singing over a prerecorded backing track as the audience crowded around.

Top of the Pops had hosted almost every great name in pop music since going on the air in 1964. The Beatles, The Stones, Bowie, Wham!, Oasis, they'd all been on to play their hits. But the program had never seen anything quite like the Spice Girls.

That no one knew quite what to make of them was obvious from the introduction they received, in which they were billed, quite seriously, as "Riot Grrls." The

Spices were still so new to the public that such a statement could be made. Of course, the connections between the band and the Riot Grrl movement were more or less nonexistent, beyond the fact that both insisted on the power of women, and in just a few short weeks, everyone would know all manner of things about the band, including their feelings about Girl Power. For now, though, confusion would have to reign, and anyone tuning in expecting to hear the dour, lo-fi alternative squalling of those Riot Grrl bands was in for a very rude awakening.

They bounced, vamped, and played to the cameras. They were eager, obviously overjoyed to be there. (And why not? This was a program on which they'd watched all their idols while growing up. It was a dream come true, just the first of many.) Mel C dressed for the occasion in a Liverpool soccer shirt, with the name of her favorite player, Steve McManaman, proudly displayed on the back. And she even did the infamous back flip, making it all look so easy.

To be fair, they didn't come across as intensely professional, seasoned performers, used to the spotlight and the adulation. They were having fun, a good time, a great laugh. And for a national debut, what could have been better? They looked like the girls next door and dressed like them. Their clothes might have been new, but there was nothing particularly fancy about them. Apart from Victoria and her love of designer labels, especially Gucci, everything could have come from any store in a British town center.

They were "Everygirl." Without saying a word, just singing, they came across as cocky, ready to take on the men at their own game, and beat them hands down. On the basis of that appearance alone, it wasn't difficult to predict that "Wannabe" was headed straight for the top.

It was a watershed moment for the Girls, in more ways than one. Sitting in their dressing room, waiting to appear, they came up with their nicknames. Geri became "Ginger Spice," although that would soon change to "Sexy Spice," as the guys began to react to her. Mel C was "Sporty Spice," Victoria "Posh Spice," Emma, the youngest, was naturally "Baby Spice," while Mel B took on the mantle of "Scary Spice." And very soon that was the way people would start referring to them.

Their three minutes on *Top of the Pops* achieved far more than publicity for the record. Before, people had only had a chance to hear them; seeing them live was a whole different matter. They were natural, rowdy, spicy. Overnight, the whole country fell in love with them. Girls found new role models, boys found some very attractive women to look at—and maybe even learn from, if they ever bothered to listen. Britain has always had a soft spot for people with a lot of spunk and cheek, particularly if they also happened to be good-looking. The Spice Girls fit the bill perfectly.

The newspapers, who just a few weeks before hadn't

wanted to know, were suddenly falling all over themselves to find out about the Spices. It wasn't just the music magazines, though, eager as they were to tell the Spicy story. That single television appearance had brought the daily tabloids in on the act. Always quick to scent out something new and lively—particularly if they could include pictures of lovely girls, preferably in states of undress—the scandal-sheet journalists were swarming.

However, while the music journalists were happy to go away with the story of the Spices as they chose to tell it, and then to print it as gospel, the tabloids wanted more, much more, on the girls themselves.

And, for the moment, the Spices were more than happy to cooperate, especially Geri, who admitted, "I can go on and on, and talk about absolutely anything to anyone."

Reporters were extremely glad to let her do just that. As "Wannabe" vaulted from the number-three slot to number one, it became nearly impossible to open a daily paper without seeing something about the Girls. Quite effortlessly, they had managed an incredible overnight transition from nobodies to pop stars to cultural phenomenon.

"As far as we're concerned, any press is good press," Victoria said later, and for now it certainly seemed true enough. They could be as outrageous as they wanted, talk about anything at all, and every word was written down. An entire population, from schoolkids to senior citizens, knew them all by name. They could identify each Spice Girl by name—and nickname.

How could it all have happened so quickly?

Part of the reason lies in the very nature of the British press, which is always on the lookout for something new, particularly if it's something they can sell to the public, or something sensational—a mixture of the two is enough to start them drooling! Doubtless they saw the Spice Girls as a flash in the pan, here today and gone tomorrow, a nine-day wonder.

There's also a tendency among British writers to build people up very quickly, making them seem wonderful and special one day, only to turn right around and tear them down the next.

Maybe they thought they'd be able to do this to the Spices. If so, they were sadly mistaken. Even as "Wannabe" reached number one for the first time, on July 27, 1996—after entering the top ten for the first time just the week before—it was apparent that the Spice Girls were going to be far more than one-hit wonders.

Being, quite literally, top of the pops was a thrill for them all. Of course it had figured in all their dreams since they got together, but having it become real was a different matter. The Girls, in Tokyo to promote the Japanese release of the single, celebrated in fine style, getting wild in a karaoke bar, Mel B swigging champagne and smoking cigars. They were number one! It was incredible, but it was also...strange.

"When I was little," Victoria mused, "I always thought, 'I want to be famous.' But you could never dream of what's happened to us. It's a bit out of the ordinary."

There was no precedent at all. It had never happened like this before, and certainly never to girls. Paricularly girls who flirted, laughed, and did things that seemed perfectly normal.

It was the first time British girls had had identifiable role models, girls who were willing and able to shout to be heard, who, much as they liked boys, didn't think they were the be-all and end-all of life. Girls who were strong and happy. Who were absolutely themselves, tattoos, piercings, and all. They could be vulgar and shock, but their sheer normality made them acceptable to everybody. They were sugar and spice, the girls who were naughty and nice.

Meanwhile the record-buying public just couldn't get enough of "Wannabe." One week at the top extended to two and three, then four, five, six, and finally seven, at which point, already pop queens of the year, they were toppled by teen idol Peter Andre (a favorite of Victoria's mother).

By then, the Spice Girls were firmly established in people's minds. They had their identities, together and alone. They were public property.

They were everywhere. Every television show wanted the Spices as guests. Apart from anything else,

"Wannabe" had galvanized the British recording industry, which was going through a very sluggish summer. The record had only been on the chart for two weeks before it claimed a gold record for sales of 400,000 copies, while two weeks later, it went platinum, outselling the number-two hit by a ratio of three to one.

By the time it dropped to number three it had topped the million mark, only the third single of 1996 to do so (the others being Babylon Zoo's "Spaceman" at the start of the year and the Fugees "Killing Me Softly"). Needless to say, Virgin Records was more than pleased. Their faith in the Spices had been amply rewarded. In the history of the company, only one other record stayed at the top of the charts for so long—Meat Loaf's "I'd Do Anything for Love (But I Won't Do That)."

The Spices had put the oomph back into British pop music. Number one with a bullet, and making history as the first British all-female group ever to hit number one. They'd wanted to break down the barriers, but this was way above everybody's expectations.

And the story was only beginning. Britain was just the tip of the iceberg. No sooner had "Wannabe" been released in other countries, the girls jetting around the world to promote it, than it was charting all over the place. Countries as far apart as Latvia and Malaysia found themselves caught in the Spicy vibe. From being the hottest thing at home, the Girls found themselves transformed into international celebrities. The demands on their time were constant. In one day they made stops in England, France, and Italy. At an in-store signing in Madrid, Spain, they found themselves mobbed by more than ten thousand fans, all trying to get pictures and autographs. Was the whole world going mad?

Well, yes. Spice mad.

In Japan, the country where they'd been working when "Wannabe" hit number one in England, the record outsold anything The Beatles had ever released, making the Spices the biggest group ever to hit those shores. The Japanese had long loved Western music, both British and American, but this was simply unbelievable. The Spices' public appearances weren't so much performances as events, with thousands crowding around trying to get close, to see and touch and talk to them.

Everywhere "Wannabe" was released, it became a hit. If any one tune could be called the song of 1996, this had to be it. No performer had ever achieved this kind of international success so rapidly before. The Beatles and Elvis, the two greatest stories of modern music, had both required a few years from their first record to become huge. To be fair, the instant global communication of today didn't exist in the fifties or sixties, but even so, no one could deny that

"Wannabe" had made the Spices into a gigantic pop phenomenon in record time.

Questions were buzzing everywhere. What song would they release next? Would it be like the first single? More importantly, would it be another smash hit, or would they end up as part of the endless stream of one-hit wonders?

That last seemed to have a pretty obvious answer. No group was going to have such a large international impact then just disappear. The world needed to brace itself: the Spice Girls were going to be around for a while.

The questions went beyond the music. In almost every country, people wanted to know about the Girls themselves, where they'd come from, what they were *really* like, who they were....

Chapter Six

Sexy Spice

So who were the Spices, anyway? In a nutshell, five cool young women from different parts of England who'd worked very hard, been very lucky, and hit a chord that resonated throughout the land. But each one had a different background and particular talents, likes, and dislikes. Each had had other jobs, ambitions, and romances.

The oldest of the Girls is Geri. Born Geraldine Estelle Halliwell on August 6, 1972, she's become known as "Sexy Spice," a nickname that evolved from the original "Ginger Spice" (bestowed on account of her red hair). With a Spanish mother, Anna Maria, who first arrived in England to work as an au pair girl (she's now a cleaner in Watford's Harlequin Centre, a job she refuses to quit, although Geri would like her to), it's perhaps not too surprising that she has a slightly exotic look, one she's not been afraid to display over the years. Her father, Lawrence, split from her mum when Geri was small, leaving the girl close to her mother, and perhaps a little bitter at her dad.

"The old-fashioned Victorian family of two-point-four kids is dead," she said. "But every child needs one decent parent and must learn honest openness about sex and tolerance."

She comes across with a cheeky poise, tattooed—on her lower back—slightly campy and trashy, but brimming with the kind of vitality, confidence, strength, and sexiness that she herself admires in other women, qualities (well, except for the sexiness) she's always seen in her heroine, Margaret Thatcher.

At five feet, two inches, she's not exactly tall, but the seventies-style platform boots she seems to favor boost her a little bit higher. With her flaming hair and blue eyes, she's developed a distinctive look for herself to match her independent personality. There's an outrageous streak in her that she'll use to tease people, to wind them up and see just how gullible they are—especially male reporters.

As she admitted to *Bikini* magazine, "Half of me can be a real nutter—I'm quite an eccentric person. In my philosophies on life, I don't like to conform to everyday life. And I think I'm quite cheeky as well. I'm naughty, but nice."

The youngest of five children (she has two brothers aged twenty-seven and twenty-nine, and two sisters aged twenty-six and thirty-one), Geri grew up in a slighty run-down brick and plaster house in Watford, a commuter town some thirty miles north of London, where there wasn't too much going on to capture her attention. The family, according to her, wasn't "very well off," and surrounded as she was by so many siblings, her assertiveness had to develop early.

"When we had cake or pudding I always had to shout louder than the others to get my share because I was the smallest."

And the smallest she seemed destined to stay. At Watford Girls' School, her classmates gave her plenty of abuse, since she proved to be a late bloomer physically, short and flat-chested until she was seventeen. When she was twelve she tried to sneak in to see Madonna's *Desperately Seeking Susan* movie, only to be turned away because she looked so young. She wanted so much to be glamorous, and fabricated tales to make herself seem more exotic, saying that she'd been born on a plane, or that the Halliwells kept sheep in their garden, anything to set herself apart. The big thing in her life was—and still is—music, and she can be quite opinionated about it.

"Pop music has been a dirty word, thanks to Kylie [Minogue] and [Stock] Aitken, and Waterman. I like the Bangles; Madonna—the way she changed her image so much; that girl from No Doubt—she's a feminist with balls. Garbage [singer Shirley Manson], I like her as well."

Madonna, in particular, proved to be something of an inspiration to young Geri, and she took the Blond One's lessons of ambition to heart.

"The way she rose from mediocrity. She wasn't a

fantastic dancer or singer, but she just used her intelligence and energy to create escapism, fantasy through art and expression. She's not that attractive, but she made herself attractive."

With the emphasis Geri has always placed on women and power, it's not a great shock that much of the Girl Power angle has come from her. Obviously, it didn't spring fully formed into her mind.

Much of it is a natural female reaction to living in a man's world, and Geri's had more contact than most of the Spices with men in power. In the late eighties, she was already on the road, not quite sure what she wanted from life beyond plenty of fun and the chance of fame. She ended up in Majorca for a while, where the dance scene was just past its peak, working in a club as a dancer.

For all that it sounded good, the job was exhausting. The visions of days lying on the beach and tanning were just that—visions. By the time her night was finished, she couldn't think of anything beyond sleeping the whole day away. There was fun, of course, but also plenty of exploitation. If she didn't do what the management said and dance herself into the ground for next to no money, there were plenty of girls more than willing to take her place. But it was also in Majorca that Geri did her first modeling, wearing a silver bikini for the photographers. That they would even ask her to pose came as a surprise.

"I never considered myself pretty enough to go in front of a camera," she admitted later.

Finally, it all became too much. She had to get out. Being adventurous, with a yen to see as much as she could of Europe before going home, there was only one destination for her—Turkey, the other side of the continent.

Arriving there, not speaking a word of Turkish, she still managed to land herself a job, and one that was much easier than dancing in clubs. Geri Halliwell was on television.

To be fair, she wasn't a star, nor likely to become one from what she was doing. Some articles have referred to her as a "TV presenter," which bends the truth a little bit. In fact, she worked on a game show. Not even as the hostess, but as one of the girls displaying the prizes contestants could win. With hair that was decidedly longer, less stylish, and a much darker shade than she wears it now, Geri would drape herself on bedroom and living-room sets, making them look all the more attractive. At the beginning of 1997, in the constant search for all things Spicy, a British television program, *The Sunday Show*, unearthed footage of Geri in her game-show role, to the delight of a nation.

But then, Geri's had the most colorful past of all the Girls. Back in England, her Turkish TV career having gone nowhere, she found herself doing all manner of boring work to pay the rent and feed herself. Cleaner (just like her mother!), barmaid, aerobics instructor—all the endurance gained from those hours of dancing had finally paid off!—she tried them all.

She couldn't believe that this was going to be her life, though, moving from one dead-end job to the next, always struggling to get by. She began answering ads in *The Stage*, one of which took her to an audition for the movie *Tank Girl* (and where, if Spice Girl mythology is to be believed, she met Victoria). There was no part in the movie for her. Indeed, luck seemed to be quite against her. In audition after audition, she was turned down.

More and more she was noticing that men always seemed to be in charge of things, making the decisions that affected her life and career. And she began to realize that the only way she could really take control of her own life was to play their game, but do it better than they ever could. If they talked, she'd shout to make herself heard. Better to be thought loud than a compliant little girl who could be used.

And if they wanted someone who was sexy, that was what she'd give them. But she wouldn't be coy; she'd be up-front about it. And so she sat for a photo session to try and become a "Page Three Girl."

It sounded sleazy, posing topless for the whole United Kingdom to leer at, but the presentation was actually anything but. The pictures were in daily, family newspapers. And after all, some of the girls who'd first come to public attention on page three had gone on to much bigger things, girls like Samantha Fox, who now had a successful recording career. The whole thing was a little nudge nudge, wink wink, but in essence it remained quite wholesome.

It seemed like the perfect new feminist gesture, in its own way. The men might be looking, but it was Geri who was really in control. And it was also a blow

against all the narrow-mindedness and sex-negative conditioning that she'd come to hate.

Above all, it could be a top laugh, and if the papers bought the pictures, there would be quite a bit of money in it for her.

The only problem was that the papers turned them down.

"I never really felt exploited at the time," she said firmly. "It was fine. I saw it for what it was."

But that was then, and this is now. Once the Spices were big news, reporters began digging round for any hidden dirt in their pasts. It didn't take long before Geri's photos surfaced—and this time there was absolutely no question that the papers would print them, under headlines that read SHE'S GERI NICE and NAUGHTY BUT SPICE! They even found their way into one of the men's magazines, which printed a whole spread, such was the new appeal of Sexy Spice.

Geri was just amused at all the attention being paid to pictures of her body.

"I've got a skin like a rhino," she said. "I've got a good sense of humor. I'm not at all embarrassed, why should I be, that's something I did, so what?"

It simply reinforced all of her opinions about men. And of the way they probably viewed her.

"I'm twenty-four," she explained to a reporter, "and it's obvious, especially with my background, I haven't gone the clean-cut way. I try to see a positive. Some of the [men] who read Page Three, I might be getting their attention and they might start listening to the music. Get some messages out. Talk about safe sex."

And she means that, too.

"I'm sure people see me as a screaming redhead with a big pair of boobs," she said, "but I like to think I've got things to say."

She can be serious when she needs to be, particularly if she's dealing with the type of males who infuriate her most, the ones with the "massive ego" that seems to be injected into them at birth. At that point, she says, she can even become "mouthy," outspoken and angry.

But give her a man who's charming, attentive, and a little bit androgynous—like the rest of the Spices, she's definitely not into guys being too macho—and that's someone she can get along with quite well.

Whether they're her style or not, the men certainly seem to go for Geri. A poll conducted by British magazine *Sky International* found her to be the most popular Spice Girl (perhaps taking the idea of "Who's Your Favorite Spice?" to extremes), with 30.8 percent of the vote. To the guys, she was the sexiest of all—which just accentuates the points she's always stressed, that men see women as a body, rather than a brain or a whole, real person. One thing she doesn't see herself as is sexy.

"It's hilarious...." she said, "I'm like any other woman in the world....I'm clumsy, not sexy....I have the same insecurities most women have....But I like that about all of us. We're proof that you don't have to be classically beautiful or six feet tall to be considered attractive....Hopefully we are role models for young girls because of that."

But even while she laughs at it, there's a little part of Geri that enjoys all the attention. She's the sort who would give a fan something from her wardrobe (in one case a pair of her hot pants), and revel in the fact that people give her tacky jewelry.

"But," she noted, "I'm quite trashy meself."

Is she? If the lads choose to end up thinking that about her, then it's the way they'd have to define themselves. Because even more than the other Girls, Geri is one of the lads, able to give and take, joke, flirt, and insult with the best of them. She can be bossy, forgetful—one of her weaknesses is that she tends to forget people's names; but given the number of people she must have met in the last year, that's hardly surprising—and thoroughly human.

She's also been the one, from the day the Spices first got together, who's been the most driven to succeed. This was her best and biggest chance to make it to the big time. Everything else had ended in failure. But while she'd tried her hand at other things, there's always been music in her life, and the chance to sing—and even more, to have some control over what she was singing—gave her the motivation to work hard. As the one with the most to overcome, having to learn how to sing in tune, she gritted her teeth and kept at it, repeating the same note over and over, the same tunes, until she'd mastered the skill. Which was typical of her. She's overcome so many barriers placed in her way because she was a woman that singing became just another hurdle to jump.

To Geri, the Spice Girls was a total commitment. A job, a good time as well, but there was always more. Not that the same wasn't true for the others, but it always seemed to be Geri who was at the forefront of things, a natural leader, perhaps partly because of her age. The others have often told Geri that her favorite saying is, "This is what we're going to do...." When Victoria and Emma wanted to go home on the weekends and visit their mums, she was the one who urged them to stay at the house in Maidenhead and keep rehearsing.

And when fame did come, so quickly, she took to it like a duck to water. She'd been waiting for this for a long, long time. There was absolutely no change in her. She was still loud, brassy Geri, the great laugh, the girl who wanted to own an Aston Martin DB6 sports car—she could probably afford a fleet of them these days—the girl with the powerful presence, who said, "Your personality is like a muscle. You have to use it."

And she flexed it often enough. She knew what she really, really wanted, and wasn't afraid to let everybody else know. She showed off her pierced belly button, flaunted her cleavage and Wonderbra. Even though she wasn't super-thin, a Kate Moss waif type, she achieved the considerable if dubious pleasure of becoming a sex symbol to thousands of guys.

The other girls all have their fans, too. Sometimes it surprises Geri and the rest of the Spices to be seen that way.

"We're not beautiful. That's something we're proud of," Mel C explained. "We're not the glamorous pop-star type that you'd expect. We're five normal girls from England...."

Like everything else, they approach fame in a humorous way. Geri knows that the music isn't high art, and makes no pretense of it being so. It's entertainment, and they do it incredibly well. They've made pop cool again.

"Pop music is about fantasy," she said, "escaping from the real world. We do things in a tongue-in-cheek way."

Even now, with the Girls on top of the world, she finds that she constantly has to prove herself, has to work to be taken seriously. Possibly the pressure is greater than ever before, with her face so well known these days. Hard as she's tried, there are still plenty of people who see her as a bimbo. Her solution? In an argument, "I throw in a lot of big words and a lot of verbal to confuse the situation."

It's a bit of a joke, but she really can do it. She's the one in the band who's always thinking and reading, the one who'll take a book by George Orwell—hardly light bedtime reading—on the road with her.

"Creatively, I love lyrics," she says. "I really do love words. My main thing in the group is I come up with ideas. I think I can talk to anybody, and I always try to understand people."

Geri is never going to be in awe of anything or anyone. If she sees a guy she likes, she's not about to wait for him to make the first move: "I go for eye contact, then I lunge...."

Always, though, it's the Spices and their career that's uppermost in her mind. All the cheek, the sass, are the coating of a girl whose last action before bed every night is to "plan the next day." She's a professional. She knows the remarkable kind of good luck the group has had, that it's hard work that will keep them at the top tomorrow and the day after. And she's determined they'll be around a lot longer than that! Being the Sexy Spice is all well and good for now. But spreading that Spice vibe and the message of Girl Power will do a great deal more good in the long run, and she knows it. Which is why she always steers interviews in that direction, even if it's not what the reporter wants to talk about.

"Our album is full of hidden messages," she told a cynical journalist from *Time Out New York*. "We're about escapism, attitude and glamour, as long as we push some sort of button."

Pushing people's buttons seems to be one of Geri's strengths, though. And for now she's very definitely pushing the right ones.

CHAPTER SEVEN

SPORTY SPICE

M el C has to be the odd one out of the Girls. While the others are more than happy to wear short skirts and hot pants, she's the one who never shows her legs, keeping them covered in sportswear—training pants, leggings, or sweats. She's also the one whose hair is usually casually pulled back in a topknot. Anyone would think that she didn't care what she looked like.

"If I left my house looking a mess and a photographer took my picture, I wouldn't care," she said firmly. "That's what I look like when I'm off to buy the milk."

Of course, it's not quite true. Whenever Melanie Jayne Chisholm appears in public, a lot of thought and effort have gone into her appearance. What seems as if it was just thrown together from her bedroom floor is actually a very carefully assembled outfit.

But that won't stop her putting on a Liverpool team shirt if she has the chance (and if not, she'll settle for the England colors). She was born in Liverpool, at

Whiston Hospital, on January 12, 1974, and her heart has remained in Merseyside ever since. Her mother, Joan, met her father at the legendary Cavern Club, where The Beatles made their famous start, and Joan sang in groups, while Mel's dad made his living as an elevator repairman for the Otis company.

Melanie was a lonely child, an only girl with two brothers, who thought for a long time that the other people she saw on the street, in the stores, and at school weren't quite real, and the family cats were her main company.

"My mum used to find me in the garage eating the cat food," she remembered. When she was young her parents divorced, and Joan took the children with her to live in Widnes, a small industrial town not far from the 'Pool, where she continued her singing and found work as a secretary in the Occupational Therapy Unit at Knowsley Metropolitan Borough Council, and eventually remarried—to Den, a man who made his living as a cabdriver, but who also played in bands. Music was always around at home, and Mel, like most kids, dreamed of being a pop star (her mother still performs in clubs, singing with a band called T Junction, who cover a lot of mainstream rock songs). For a while she wanted to be just like singer Neneh Cherry and, when she was fifteen, permed her hair into an Afro, from which she insists it's never recovered. There was even a vague interest in acting when she was very young. But even then, it was apparent that Mel didn't quite fit in with the other girls in her class.

"I always ended up playing a sheep at the Nativity play while the other girls dressed as angels," she recalled. "I didn't mind, though, in fact I'd rather have played Joseph."

Growing up, she also studied ballet for three years, with the hope of becoming a dancer. At five feet, six inches, she had a chance, but the opportunities just didn't run her way. She auditioned for the musical *Cats*, and came close but didn't make it, ending up working in a fish-and-chip shop while trying to get gigs as a session singer.

"She was a very good actress but was known for her singing," one old friend said. "Mel just wanted to perform in any way she could. She was destined to be famous."

Unfortunately, destiny eluded her until she answered the ad for girls who could sing and dance in *The Stage*.

The Girl nicknamed "Sporty Spice" has always been a fitness fanatic. A nonsmoker, she's the girl who always likes to be doing *something*, who has to be in motion, whether it's jogging, working out at the gym—the last thing she does at night is exercise, performing fifty stomach crunches—or taking part in some sport, like training with Rickmansworth Ladies soccer club, which she had to stop doing once fame began and recognition from fans began to break up the team's training sessions, much to the annoyance of the other team members.

So now she has to content herself with supporting the Liverpool football team. But with her schedule, that tends to be limited to watching them on television. Still, that doesn't stop her wishing for more, like being able to take part in a Liverpool training session (and being recognized as exactly the player the squad was looking for), or, best of all, sharing a postgame bath with the team, even if she'd "make sure I had something on...I'm not *that* kind of girl!"

It says a great deal about her fanatical support for the club that her favorite song is "You'll Never Walk Alone," which has been sung for so long on the terraces of Anfield, Liverpool's stadium, that it's become the club's unofficial anthem. These days, of course, Mel C is famous enough to be invited to spend time with the players, and when that invitation comes from Jamie Redknapp, one of Liverpool's young forwards, it's too good to turn down.

"He's gorgeous," she enthused. "Whenever he speaks to me I just go to pieces. Recently he's been looking even more gorgeous with his long hair. Ooh God."

But when she does have the chance to go to a game, it's definitely to watch, and not to be watched. Last year, having seen her team win at home, she said, "After the final whistle blew, they started playing 'Wannabe' over the PA, it was really embarrassing."

At heart she's still the fan, the ordinary girl who just happened to make it big. She's the one with the nose ring and the two tattoos, a Chinese ideogram on her shoulder, depicting the characters for woman and strength ("so it sort of *says* 'Girl Power'"), and a Celtic band tattooed on her right arm, a design that looks particularly good when she's flexing her biceps—a technique she uses to attract men.

After doing this, she'll say, "I've got two tickets for a Liverpool match, do you fancy coming?"

These days, however, the chances of her actually going up to someone and saying that are quite slim, given that she's "quite shy and I find it difficult approaching guys."

But when it's a man who's interested in her, her advice is, "You won't get me on your side by asking me to a fancy restaurant or any of that sissy stuff. What would interest me is an invitation to a football match."

The woman lives, eats, and breathes the game! When she's not too busy being one of the Spices, that is. Actually, it's more than just the team—she simply loves Liverpool and everything to do with it, even the English soap opera *Brookside*, which is set there, because "All those [Liverpool] accents make me feel better whenever I get homesick."

If Geri's the Spice who advocates political and professional equality for women, Mel C's the one who'd like to be physically equal. She'd like to be able to bench-press as much weight and develop muscles the way men do.

Geri has characterized her as a woman who "will always look after you. She carries your bag if it's too heavy. She's a really nice person, but tough, too. She's the silent but deadly type." Perhaps she's not quite as boisterous and outspoken as the rest of the Girls, but just like the others, Mel C is quite aware of the problems girls face in the world, and the way they're reacting to them.

"There is a new attitude," she said. "Girls are taking control. If you want to wear a short skirt, then you go on and wear it. You should wear what you want," and, naturally, you should never be judged by your clothes.

Emma sees her as a person who's "very fit and funny. She's a very funny person when you talk to her, and when she's got something to say, it's very important. And she gets us up and going when we've been a bit lazy, all of us, she gets us up, saying, 'Come on now, we've got a singing lesson, or we've got to have a dance lesson.' She's a cool chick."

But Mel C's a cool chick with more than a few insecurities. She sees herself as the "plain one" of the group, and she has her share of neuroses.

"All the tins of baked beans in my kitchen cupboards have to face the same way," she admitted, "and there always have to be four tins, and if not, definitely an even number."

Strange? Yes, but who isn't in her own way?

With a year that's been "totally messed up *mad*...the craziest year of our lives," Mel C remains a girl who'd prefer to order Chinese even when the best and most expensive foods in the world are hers for the asking. Her feet, in their sneakers, are planted very firmly on the ground.

Fame hasn't gone to her head—all the Girls seem incredibly sane, considering what the last twelve months have been like for them—and she knows it's not the be-all and end-all of life.

"I know it sounds ungrateful," she said, "but sometimes fame isn't that much fun. You're visiting all these fantastic places and you'll be sitting there moaning, 'I want to go home.'"

Fame has its price. And sometimes it had to be hard for the Girls to see just how big they've become.

"When it all started, you couldn't get your head round it," Mel C said. "But now we realize you don't have to get your head round it."

That's quite true for all of them. Still, life on the road can become overwhelming. Sometimes too overwhelming. When the Spices were in Portugal, attending yet another promotional party to publicize *Spice*, "we were all desperate to go home," Victoria remembered. Head of Virgin Records "Richard Branson was there too, so Emma said to him: 'Um, how are you getting home tonight?' And he goes, 'In my private jet.' So she goes, 'Can we get a lift?'"

What choice did he have but to say yes? When it's

all too much, there's nothing like the comfort of home. And for Mel, that's where the heart is. The first thing she did after getting home from an exhausting tour of Japan was to go spend some time with her mum.

Musically she does like things other than "You'll Never Walk Alone," although no other song—not even one she herself has helped make famous—is likely to replace it in her affections.

"Yeah, I've got different tastes," she says, "but at the moment I'm really into the Britpop scene—you know, Blur, Oasis, Supergrass. I kinda like all the big guitar bands, but my favorite artist of all time is Stevie Wonder. But I'm a big Madonna fan as well, so it varies."

She even likes, believe it or not, Bruce Willis. Not so much as an actor, but as a musician, going so far as to confess that she owns his *Return of Bruno* album, the sort of information most people would keep hidden in a very dark corner.

To Mel C, the Spices stand as a very positive alternative to all the negativity that music's seen in recent years, "with the grunge scene and gangsta rap and stuff like that. What we're about is having a laugh and having fun, and I think people enjoy seeing other people enjoying themselves."

Enjoying herself means—other than being onstage—being at home, watching cooking shows on television, or trying to go grocery shopping unnoticed at her local supermarket. She likes her apartment to be clean, but hates anything to do with housework. At night she might change out of her sweats and into combat pants to go clubbing with a couple of the other Girls—these days, they're all VIP guests everywhere, treated like royalty—but even then, she doesn't overdo things. Some dancing and a couple of drinks is her limit. Fitness comes first to Mel. Every morning she's up early to jog, even on tour, when she makes sure to pack her favorite running shoes.

In spite of all the good things she projects, Mel C doesn't seem to be much of a favorite with the guys. In the *Sky International* "Who's Your Favorite Spice Girl?" poll, she came a resounding last with only 6.5 percent of the vote.

Why?

It's a good question, and the answer has to do with her image. Whereas Geri is all-out sexy, Emma sweet, Victoria sultry, and Mel B just plain wild, Mel C is kinetic, always moving, kicking out, dancing, doing her famous back flip. You're not going to see her in a short skirt. She doesn't show her cleavage (in fact she jokes that her favorite country is Holland, because "it's flat, just like me"). She's as close as any of the Spices are likely to come to quiet and serious.

Her physicality, the way she hides herself in almost anything made by Adidas, sets her well apart from the others.

"Sometimes I feel like a bit of a spare part," she

admitted. "I'm the one in the corner." Still, it seems that shyness can have its advantages. While the cameras are squarely aimed at the others, "I'm the one the paparazzi don't follow. Touch wood."

And perhaps the men see her more as a sister than a possible girlfriend. In some ways, she's more like them, ready to talk about soccer at the drop of a hat, not afraid of decking someone in an argument, if it becomes *absolutely* necessary.

"I'm the minder," she admits. "Me and Mel B compete to see who's the hardest—we're like the Gallagher brothers [from Oasis]."

All the emphasis the media has placed on sex and the Spice Girls annoys her.

"I find it frustrating sometimes," she admitted, "and we've had a lot recently, where things just get reverted round to sex all the time...and a lot of innuendos and stuff...we're not about sex. It might come into the equation....I mean, when people treat us as a product, and we sell sex. And we don't sell sex. We write music."

While she may not be the most popular with the male population, there are those who consider Mel C to be the real brains, and perhaps even the soul, of the Spice Girls. According to Ian Lee, who worked at Trinity Studios, where the girls initially practiced, when Geri and Mel B asserted their strong personalities, and fought "like cat and dog...Mel C would always act as the peacemaker." Lee also called her "the real talent in the band," although he noted wryly that she'd "spend all her spare time watching football."

Mel's role as the peacemaker has continued, although these days the Spices are very much the best of friends. Diplomacy remains her strong suit, and when the disputes do occur—as they're almost bound to, in one way or another—she's the one who plays devil's advocate, who can see both sides of the question, and can sort it all out amicably, which, as Emma pointed out, "is annoying if you want her to stick up for you."

She fully understands the tide of popularity, up one minute, down the next. And while the Spices have a very serious message in Girl Power, she doesn't want anyone to take the band too seriously.

"We never mean to offend or hurt anybody. We're just a bit naughty." She's even concerned that they might be getting too much exposure. "Eventually, it will probably get boring. And we don't want people thinking, 'Oh, the Spice Girls are on telly again—I bet they have had a food fight.'"

For herself, work has been the main thing in her life ever since the Spices got together. She doesn't have a boyfriend, and hasn't for years, although the tabloids did track down some of the boys she dated when she was a teenager. There was Ian McKnight, a boy from her school whom she met when they took part in a school play. After he dumped her, she took up with his younger brother Keith, in an attempt to make Ian jealous. That didn't work, but Mel C and Keith ended up close friends. Once he was out of the romantic picture, Mel met Ryan "Raz" Wilson, who became her boyfriend for a few months, until they just drifted apart. As it stands now, though, she can't even remember her last date, because "it's so long ago that it's embarrassing." And that's the way it's likely to remain, at least for the foreseeable future.

"At the moment my career is my priority, but I don't want to be with anyone in the industry. I want to have un-popstar boyfriends."

Even if she isn't Britain's favorite Spice Girl, there probably aren't many guys who'd turn her down.

CHAPTER EIGHT

POSH SPICE

To call Victoria (and it's always Victoria, never *ever* Vicky or Vicki) Addams "Posh Spice" is just right. Because the real lay-dee of the band, the sultry Girl with the intense look, really does come from a rich family. Even so, it's perhaps not too astonishing that she ended up pursuing music, since her dad, Tony, had tried his hand at pop himself, playing in a sixties band called the Sonics, who covered Beatles' songs as well as writing their own.

At the time it seemed as if stardom beckoned, but after their manager died, it all fell apart. Disenchanted, Victoria's father quit showbiz and turned to business instead, starting a wholesale electrical-equipment company.

It turned out to be a very good move, and soon he was making more money than he'd ever thought possible. Certainly enough to let him move his family out to the "Home Counties," that expensive belt of land outside London populated by the rich, titled, and, yes, pop stars. Settling in an extensive, wood-beamed property (which cost almost half a million pounds) in the village of Goff's Oak, Hertfordshire (where they shared a gardener with the Queen Mother), he continued adding to the bank account. Meanwhile his wife, Jackie, busied herself with their three children, Victoria, who arrived in the world on April 7, 1975, her siblings Louise (now nineteen) and Christian (now seventeen), and their three Yorkshire terriers (Bambi, Truffle, and Lucy).

"The house is supposed to be haunted," Victoria said. "My mum used to see the bottom half of a schoolmistress walking up the stairs! We thought originally she had senile dementia, because it runs in Mum's family, but then my dad saw it as well."

From an early age she shared her dad's fascination with music and dancing, and as soon as she could walk, she was dancing in the living room with her father, with Stevie Wonder's "Sir Duke" as the sound track.

In school, she was very much a good kid who studied hard.

"I was really boring at school," she admitted. "I did all my homework on time and passed all my exams."

The teachers liked her, calling her "pleasant and pretty." That popularity didn't extend as far as the other kids, however. They saw Victoria as a Goody Two-shoes, a very timid, shy girl who just wanted to keep herself on the straight and narrow.

"I was probably one of the most unpopular kids

you'd ever have at school," she said, looking back. Not being invited along left her feeling very isolated and lonely, with few friends; all too often she'd end up in the girls' bathroom, crying her eyes out.

Even in a very well-to-do area, her father's wealth stood out, especially when he'd drop the children off at school in his Rolls-Royce. Kids being what they are, Victoria was given a rough time about it, so much that she'd beg her dad to take her instead in the old truck he used for deliveries.

School was really little more than a nightmare of bullying for her.

"For a while I was a complete wreck," she revealed to *Sugar* magazine. "I remember I'd go to classes and be petrified. I'd usually get pushed around and sworn at, then the girls who did it would say things like, 'We're gonna get you after school.'" While they never actually beat up on her, there was plenty of shoving, and she came to realize that "sometimes mental bullying is worse than physical bullying."

Away from all that, Victoria could come alive and really be herself, filling much of her free time with music. Her first pop crush was on Bros, the boy group originally managed by the Herberts and Chic Murphy, who'd bring the Spices together. In particular, Victoria loved Matt Goss.

"I thought he was really sexy," she said.

She bought all the records, put his pictures in scrapbooks, knew everything about him, and went to the

Bros concerts, where she screamed along with all the other girls.

She was in love with him. In real life, though, romance wasn't quite so easy for a young Victoria, who found herself dating a vicar's son. While she dressed to kill, he'd arrive in a *Star Wars* T-shirt and sneakers that fastened with Velcro straps—hardly the height of fashion!

"He looked a right state," she said sadly, "but he redeemed himself when he gave me a silver cross—but I found out later that his dad had bought them in bulk and he had nicked one."

And that was the end of that.

The interest in dance that she'd cultivated as a child continued. Much as she adored Matt, there was also ballet dancer Rudolf Nureyev and Leroy from the television series *Fame* to look up to and

idolize. When Victoria was eight, she pestered her mum for dance lessons, until Jackie finally gave in and enrolled her daughter at the Jason Theatre School, run by Joy Spriggs.

"The very first time I saw Victoria dance I knew she was special," Spriggs said later. "She won so many medals and stayed at the theater....Victoria ate, slept, and drank dancing."

She was good enough that she managed to secure herself a place at the Laine Theatre Arts School in Surrey to further her studies. Unhappy at school, she jumped at this chance. The three-year course proved to be a completely different world, a revelation to her.

Jackie Addams could say of her daughter, "All Victoria ever wanted to do was dance," but now she really had the chance to make it *all* she did. At five feet, six inches, she was tall enough to be considered as a possible professional dancer. And she loved it. After being so miserable at school, she suddenly found herself enjoying every minute of college.

Away from home for the first time, she lived in "digs," renting a room in a private house with a landlady who cooked meals and kept a watchful eye on her—Victoria was still only sixteen, after all.

She was luckier than most students, having wealthy parents who saw that she wanted for nothing financially. From an early age, she'd always dressed nicely—"She was always really well turned out," as one teacher recalled—and the pleasure she took in good clothes had now become a love of designer labels, none of which were cheap. Armani suits, Versace, and particularly Gucci, they were all there in her wardrobe.

But even if she dressed the part of the little rich girl among a bunch of slobby students, at Laine, for the first time in her life, Victoria felt part of the crowd. During her three years there, she made more friends than she had in ten years of regular school. Those painful memories still flood over her sometimes, to the point where she's said, "You look back now and think, 'I'd love to be stuck in that room with all those kids that said all those things about me.'"

College, though, was nothing but a good time. Even the hard work was enjoyable, and the nights, out clubbing with the girls, were an endless blur of fun.

Still, all things have to come to an end, and eventually Victoria graduated, finding herself living in a very tough world. There was a job with a touring theater company, but for the most part work was difficult to come by. She was just one of many hopefuls auditioning for parts, another face among thousands.

Until she answered the ad in *The Stage* for girls who could sing and dance to form a pop group. It seemed absolutely perfect for her—the three things Victoria had always loved.

Still, even after being chosen, things didn't always go smoothly for her. She worked every bit as hard as the others, but with her family living close by, she liked to go home every weekend to relax and spend

SPICE *Girls*

Emma

Baby Spice

Geri

Sexy Spice

Scary Spice

Mel C

SPICE Girls

Sporty Spice

Victoria

PoSh SpiCe

SPICE Girls

time with them, something that annoyed Geri for a while.

Once that was all sorted out, though, the girls got along like a house on fire, and Victoria, who'd always been a little reserved around others after her experiences at school, really began to loosen up and become one of the Girls. Even her upper-crust inhibitions began to fall by the wayside, and soon she was almost as wild as the others—almost. There was still a little something that held her back at times. She rarely drank—the others had forced champagne on her when they celebrated their signing with Virgin Records—and still kept her emotions inside.

But the Spice spirit could be very infectious, and by the time they were international stars, Victoria was up for a laugh just as much as Geri, Emma, Mel B, or Mel C.

"The most outrageous thing I've ever done was flashing to a lift full of tourists when we were staying in a hotel in America," she admitted. "I was running around the corridors just wearing a dressing gown, so when the doors opened I flashed."

Outrageous? Of course. But still very innocent, like girls on vacation doing silly things for the fun and on a dare.

Victoria may assert that she's not really posh, but her mum was very happy with the nickname she was given.

"My mum loves me being called Posh Spice—she's hoping to become known as Posh Mum!"

The massive success of the Spice Girls has made Victoria an internationally known face, just like the others. And it's given her all the wealth she needs to indulge her lavish tastes—something she's more than happy to do. While she doesn't have any tattoos or piercings on her flesh (and is highly unlikely ever to get any—it's just not posh), she did have one of her fingernails pierced, and a diamond stud inserted. And she's probably one of the few people in the world to own a custom-made Armani toe ring.

The big joy of the money, though, is that she can now shop anywhere and everywhere she wants. "The others really make fun of me about it," she confessed, "but I just love designer clothes."

And nearly as much fun as owning them is going shopping for them. Wherever the Girls travel—and by now they've covered most parts of the globe—Victoria is determined to find some time to hit the stores. At home in London, she likes to pass her time and credit cards in Harrods and the extremely swanky Harvey Nichols.

"Harrods is posher, but Harvey Nichols has more style" is her considered opinion. But above both of them she prefers the very fancy Prada, where she's been known to spend $3,000 on a purse.

All this might seem incredibly frivolous, but there's a deeper side to Victoria as well. She boasts that she

only reads *Elle* and that "I've never in my life succeeded at reading a book from cover to cover!" but
there's still plenty going on in her mind. Like the
other Spices, she's a strong proponent of Girl Power.
Her politics veer toward the conservative—which isn't
too astonishing, given her moneyed upbringing—but
she's thought about what she wants, and what's
important to her. Money can buy a lot of things, but
happiness isn't one of them.

And that's definitely also true of romance. Given
Victoria's extravagant tastes, she might be expected to
date someone rich—another pop star, perhaps.
(Certainly her mother would love her to date British
hitmaker Peter Andre. Jackie's a big fan of his, with
pinups all over the house, much to Victoria's embar-
rassment, since she has to see them when she's at
home, where she still lives. And it's been said that
Peter definitely fancies Victoria.) Or possibly a business-
man, someone in her own financial league. She's said
any number of times that she likes men in good, taste-
ful clothing, as long as they also remember that shoes
are important, too (and how many of them do?). But
proving that opposites attract, as it turns out, her
boyfriend, twenty-two-year-old Stuart Bilton, is cur-
rently unemployed. And it's a very serious love match.

"They're talking about getting engaged," one friend
said. "Victoria's mad about Stuart. They're always
together whenever she's home."

There's a vast difference between the sixty dollars a

week that Stuart receives as an unemployment check and the thousands that are pouring into Victoria's bank account, and it's a credit to her that she can see past the career to the man. But it's not something she chooses to talk about, preferring to keep her private life very remote from the public gaze.

"I don't talk about my relationships," she explained. "I might have a boyfriend, but I never tell anyone. It's not easy having relationships in this business."

He's undoubtedly someone who can make Victoria smile, which is something she doesn't do too often in public. It's not pouting, and it's certainly not boredom. She simply believes that a moody, slightly serious look is more flattering to her than a big grin—unusual in a performer—but it seems to work. The men definitely fall for it in droves. In the *Sky International* poll, Victoria came in a close second as favorite Spice Girl (after Geri), with 28.6 percent of the vote.

It's a cool, aloof sexiness that she projects, but without ever being haughty. And it's something of a mask, since Victoria herself is actually shy. Out with the other Girls, she can get a little carried away and forget that reserve, but alone it takes her over.

"I never chat up guys," she admitted. "If I was with the girls, I'd walk up to them and wink because the girls give me confidence, but on my own I go all shy."

All right, so it's not quite Girl Power in action, but that's just the way she is. Certainly in every other way she's a strong, assertive woman, the type who won't take anything from anybody, who'll stand up for equality (except in housework, which she's more than happy to let a man do for her), the right to do, say, and think exactly what she wants.

Like the rest of the Spices, at work Victoria is a consummate professional. The overwhelming, rowdy, girl-gang appearance can be deceptive. Behind the loudness, each of them has an overwhelming desire to see the Spice Girls succeed. Even now, when they're international superstars, there's still more. The chance to tour properly and perform, to make more albums. The chance to really have an impact.

Growing up and buying Bros records, Victoria could only imagine what fame might be like. It was something distant, something to be hoped for but unlikely to be achieved. These days she's eclipsed anything and everything Bros managed to achieve. And the journey's still only just beginning. There might already be a whole generation of girls growing up and looking forward to dressing in designer suits and fancy shoes, pushing their way through life without ever smiling.

So maybe it's a slightly different Spice vibe than the others (she calls it paprika), a little more introspective and a little quieter. It just goes to prove that there's room for every girl in there.

CHAPTER · NINE

BABY SPICE

To look at Emma Bunton, you'd think she was nothing more than a sweet, innocent, and completely defenseless girl. Which simply goes to show how deceptive appearances can be. Yes, she's cute, and she's the baby of the bunch—hence the nickname "Baby Spice" (or, when she wears her hair in bunches, "Angelica," after the character on the *Rugrats* cartoon series)—but she can also be a little devil, and she's very far from defenseless. In fact, she could beat most people in a fight, since she's a blue belt at Goju, a variation of karate, a sport she learned from her black-belt mother, Pauline, who teaches it (and who passed on a few basic moves to the rest of the Spices).

It was Emma who taught the others the karate kicks they used in the video for "Say You'll Be There."

And it's Emma who can find—or sometimes start—the biggest trouble of any of the Spices. She's the one who'll streak in a hotel corridor (although the incident was nowhere near as public as the newspapers made it out to be), then turn on a sweet smile and talk her way out of it.

"She gets away with murder," Mel B said. "She's like one of those children who's really naughty and then gives you a kiss."

You just can't stay mad at her.

But growing up, Emma Lee Bunton, born on January 21, 1976, never really had the time to be bad. She was always too busy. Her father, Trevor, was a milkman, and a young Emma would sometimes go on his route with him, helping deliver the bottles.

But it was her mother that Emma was closer to, and still is.

"My mum is my idol," she said. "I love her more than anything in the whole world." And it really is true. When she's out on the road, Emma will call home two or three times a day to chat with Pauline or her younger brother, PJ.

"We're like best buddies," is how Emma described her mum. "I really miss her when I go away."

The Spices' fame is very recent, but it's far from being the first time that Emma's been in the spotlight. When she was three, and on vacation with her parents, Pauline entered her in a beauty contest. Emma easily won, and her folks, who already thought she was lovely, began to realize that other people might feel the same way.

So once they were home again, photographs were

taken, and Pauline began to make the rounds of the modeling agencies, trying to find work for her daughter. It wasn't long before the Norrie Carr group signed her up, and Emma had her own agent, Gill Peters.

"Emma was a hit," Peters recalled. "She never stopped working and had that special something that we were looking for. She had a twinkle in her eye and loved the camera."

And the camera loved her right back. By the time she was five, Emma was getting regular jobs as a model for the Mothercare catalog (clothing for babies and young children), making thirty dollars an hour, while attending the Kay School of Dance in Finchley, her native part of North London. To her at the time it wasn't modeling, though. She called it, quite aptly, "smiles."

That was just the start. Print work led to television, and soon Emma was known in Britain as the Polly Pocket Toy girl, the Mentadent B toothpaste girl, and the Nestlé white chocolate girl. She even advertised travel cards (rail discount cards). In Switzerland, she was the girl who ate strawberries.

She was quite famous, very young. But amazingly, it didn't go to her head—that wasn't part of her personality, and her parents wouldn't have allowed it to happen, anyway. Instead, she became something of a big sister to the models who were even younger than her.

"She was very professional," said Crystal Power, who worked with Emma on the Mothercare catalog.

"If the little ones cried, Emma gave them a hug and told them that everything would be all right."

It seemed quite obvious that Emma was destined for a showbiz career, so Trevor and Pauline decided to prepare her properly by sending her to a stage school, the Sylvia Young Stage School in Islington, London, where dance, drama, and singing—every aspect of performance—became her life.

"She loved singing and dancing," one of her teachers remembered. "And she was very good at them. She always had a smile on her face and got on well with her peers."

When Emma was eleven, her parents decided to split up. Quite naturally, Emma stayed with Pauline, while Trevor moved out of the house.

"Everyone says, 'It was the worst time of my life,' but it wasn't, really," she said. She still had school, her dreams of real stardom, and alone in her room she could record her own radio shows on a cassette recorder. With her friends, she'd hold Madonna parties, where every girl had to dress like Madonna and mime to the records, using a hairbrush as a microphone. And there was even a first boyfriend and a first kiss, when Emma was thirteen, and dated a boy for a whole week. But love wasn't all she'd hoped it would be.

"The kiss was a complete disaster. His lips were completely rough and he had bad breath." Needless to say, it didn't last too long after *that*.

Still, as long as there was school, her world still had a center of sorts. But when Emma turned fourteen, that was pulled from her. Trevor and Pauline, who, although separated, had been paying for Emma to attend Sylvia Young, simply didn't have the money anymore. Emma would have to leave.

"It just sort of went all wrong," she said. "It was awful."

She started classes at a normal school and hated them. She felt totally out of place there. She knew it, and so did the other girls. Luckily, this gig didn't turn out to be for too long. Just three weeks after Emma had been forced to leave Sylvia Young, the school wrote and offered her a full scholarship. Perfectly happy, Emma returned.

Even then, grateful as she was, she could still play her pranks. In her last year at the school, one day she stuffed all the sinks in the girls' rest room with toilet paper and left the faucets running, causing a huge flood.

It was at Sylvia Young, where Emma studied for her BTEC certificate, that Pepi Lemer gave her voice lessons, a connection that would prove very useful a year or two later.

Initially, Emma applied to get into college to study drama, even though, as she said, "I was always more into singing and dancing." But when no place was offered to her, she knew it was time to start hitting the audition circuit. Like all the other kids there, she'd done some acting at Sylvia Young, taking part in school and class plays. Now she was forced to take it all more seriously.

However, in spite of the sweet smile and charming looks, the offers didn't come flooding in. There was a very brief appearance as an extra on a cop show, *The Bill*, and then she tried out for a role on one of the highly rated British soap operas, *Eastenders*, and "I got down to about the last six girls for the part of Bianca," but she lost out in the end.

So it was back to open calls, and finding whatever work she could to make ends meet. At least living wasn't too expensive, since she stayed with her mother and brother at their Finchley flat (where she still lives, although she could afford somewhere much better). And that was the way things stayed until Pepi managed to track her down and Emma strutted her stuff as a Spice Girl.

Even after the call and audition, Pauline didn't quite know what to make of the group her daughter would be joining.

"In the beginning," Emma says, laughing, "my mum said, 'What is this, a religious cult or something?' And the truth is that's how it's worked out— we're like a religious cult."

Well, these days there are certainly a lot of people who worship them. But back then the future was a lot cloudier. Emma found that she fit in very well with the rest of the crew. Away from home for the first time, she could be as loud and wild as the best of them, do the most outrageous things, and then escape all the blame.

"Emma might portray herself as being the sweet and innocent Spice, but it's not true," Geri insisted. "Me and Mel B always get the blame for her pranks."

With her very girly style of short skirts, baby-doll dresses, and hair either pulled crammed into pigtails or combed with straight bangs, she certainly looked the part of "Baby Spice." Butter wouldn't have melted in her mouth.

Maybe not butter, but doughnuts certainly would. Because Emma, tiny as she is, happens to love them— but only the sugarcoated variety. To her, anything else just isn't a real doughnut. Her ambition (although it's hard to take it seriously) is to be able to eat a hundred doughnuts in a sitting. Then again, she's also claimed, with a very straight face, that she wears leather underwear.

Something far more realistic, and much more truthful, is to simply have a very good time with the fame the Spices have received. That can include getting very rowdy—as in the now infamous streaking incident.

A few reports said that Emma, Mel B, and Geri streaked through the lobby of the Los Angeles hotel where they were staying. Like so much you read in the papers, it was a bit of an exaggeration. The Girls *did* streak—they've never denied that for a minute, in fact they're quite proud of it—but it was in the corridor outside their rooms, just on a dare, and no one else was around to see them.

For all of Emma's craziness, as the youngest, the others look after her. She might have been in show business longer than the rest, but they're older, and possibly a little wiser.

"The other girls have taught me a lot about growing up," she admitted, "and I know I probably still have a lot to learn, both personally and professionally."

The way it's all exploded so quickly leaves her, just like the other Spices, absolutely amazed.

"To have got this far by twenty seems like a miracle. I have always dreamed of fame and a career in pop or showbiz, so to have a taste of it at my age is a fantasy come true."

And the last few months have been far more than a taste of fame. As the little girl of the bunch, Emma could have been forgiven for letting it go to her head, to have become snooty and arrogant. But that hasn't been the case. Although she knows that "I can be a real brat sometimes," the others won't let her head get too big, and besides, as she told Smash Hits, "My mum taught me to be polite to people even if they weren't nice to you because that raises you above their level."

Inevitably, of course, the Spices argue. They spend so much time together, and they're such very different people, that the rows are certain to happen, especially when you factor in all the pressure they've been under. It might sound like the perfect life, jetting from country to country, receiving all kinds of adulation, but in reality it can be incredibly stressful. Success has torn bands apart before. But if that should ever happen to the Spice Girls, it won't be Emma who quits.

"I would never go solo. I love being in a band because it's like being with my...best mates and having a laugh every day. We're like sisters, I love them all so much."

She's the Spice that most girls can identify with, the one who seems so *normal*, just like the girl next door. Her little-girl dresses seem to have come straight off the racks of department stores, not ahead of fashion, not even anything special, but clothes anyone could and would buy. Even the colors—pinks and whites, with purple for special occasions—are quite ordinary. She's cute, but not beautiful, her hair is cut very simply. But that's the way it should be. Emma's philosophy for the Girls is, "With us, what you see is what you get," and it's quite true for all of them. It's not just her—every one of them is a very real, genuine person.

Understandably, she also has her male admirers. The *Sky International* poll found her to be the third most popular Spice Girl among men, coming in with a total of 25.3 percent of the vote. And it was recently revealed that Emma has a fan in very high places indeed—Prince William of Gloucester, the older son of Prince Charles and Lady Di, the boy who might well become king one day. He studies at Eton, the famous private school, and recently took down his Pamela

Anderson poster, replacing it with a picture of Emma.

Needless to say, Emma was surprised and flattered when the news leaked to the papers (and appeared under the headline WHAT WILLS ROYALLY ROYALLY WANTS). The others teased her, suggesting that she might start receiving invitations to Buckingham Palace.

"It was quite weird, actually," she said. "I was quite gobsmacked [surprised]. Especially taking Pam down and putting me up. I was 'Hold on a minute—it's not real.'" Still, even though he's in line for the throne, and one of the most powerful lads in the land, a true Spice Girl wasn't about to let herself be in awe of a boy. "But he's not the most gorgeous person in the world, is he?" she added.

Nor is he the only member of royalty to like the Spices. Sarah Ferguson, better known to the world as Fergie, might not quite be part of the Royal Family anymore, but her position is close enough, and *she's* a big fan of the Girls—she even went out and bought the *Spice* album. But then again, maybe that's not too surprising—at heart, she's always been a Spice Girl herself, doing what she wanted, being proud of who she is, and not caring what anyone else thinks. Girl Power in very blue-blooded action (even more upper-class than Victoria!).

By Christmas 1996, it had all become too much for Emma and the others. The Spices had worked so hard and achieved so much that they all needed a break, some time to go on vacation and get out of the public eye for a few weeks.

During their time off, Emma took her mother to the Caribbean, to a resort in Barbados.

But it was Emma's twenty-first birthday party that proved to be a huge success, prompting Emma to say, "The best thing about getting home is meeting up with your mates."

Naturally, all the Spices were there, and stayed until three A.M., when Pauline decided it was time for Emma to go home. Geri, as you might expect, wasn't yet finished for the night, and while Emma was back in Finchley, climbing into her pajamas, Geri was on her way to yet another party.

But when Pauline said it was time to leave, there was no way Emma could refuse her—even if it was her big do.

"Emma does everything she tells her," a friend revealed. "Her private life is as dull as a garden catalog."

Dull in a lot of ways, but certainly not without its share of romance. She has a huge crush on *ER*'s George Clooney; some of her girlfriends think he's far too old, but to Emma "he's a real man." In real life, though, what she likes is for "boys to look cute and naughty, but I want a good friend, too." She prefers her guys to be "clean-cut. I've always gone for real blokes like bricklayers. I'm not into showbiz types." And it seems as though she might have found the ideal person.

Mark Vergueze is the same age as Emma, and he definitely isn't a showbiz type. He works as a dental technician. But he did get a small taste of the high life when Emma took him along on the family vacation to Barbados. A small taste was all it was, though.

"People think that as the boyfriend of a Spice Girl I sit around all day playing pool," he said. "But I work very hard. Emma makes it all worthwhile, though."

Unfortunately, the way her life is at the moment, Emma and Mark aren't able to spend too much time together.

"I don't see him very much these days because I'm always away," she explained. "I love it when I go home, 'cos he just can't relate to what I do at all, he just relates to me. When we get together we don't even talk about the group."

With her love life settled, Emma's free to really help push the Girls. Even with three number-one hits in England, and "Wannabe" topping the charts in so many countries—not to mention the phenomenal success of *Spice*—they've really only just scratched the surface of their abilities.

"We've only had a bit of success, so maybe it's good that we don't get sucked into the fame thing. If we stopped to think about it, we'd be in a mess."

With their feet planted on the ground, there's still so much left to achieve, not the least of which is broadening the message of Girl Power. To Emma,

that means, "You can be a strong female, and wear makeup and a Wonderbra!"

It's about being exactly who you want to be, and taking absolutely no notice of what other people say.

To many, Emma could be nothing more than a cute, fluffy blonde, a bimbo or an airhead with a lovely smile and a lot of luck. There are plenty who'd say that—there are always people who resent it when others are successful—but she doesn't care. Especially if they're male.

"We're not trying to be sex symbols for boys," she said. "We want to show girls that if we can make it, so can they!"

So however much they pose for the boys and the photgraphers, that's the heart of the message: inspiring girls to get out there and do it for themselves, to be as strong as the Spices, to look as pretty as they want; in short, to be themselves, and not let any man tell them who, how, or what they should be.

And just because someone like Emma has a talent for singing the high parts, the harmonies, is called Baby Spice, and looks and dresses like a girly girl, it would be a major mistake not to take her seriously. As with all the Spices, there's a lot going on. And the boys really need to remember who has the blue belt in Goju...just because she can smile sweetly doesn't mean she can't pack a punch as well.

CHAPTER · TEN

SCARY SPICE

Some people wouldn't think "Scary Spice" the most flattering of nicknames. Mel B's mother, Andrea, is certainly one of them. However, Mel herself just laughs it off. She knows what it really means. And she also knows that the Spice who can come on strongest of them all is herself capable of being scared—by spiders.

Melanie Janine Brown was born on the May 29, 1975, in the Burley area of Leeds, Yorkshire, an industrial town in the north of England. Her father, Martin, was one of many who moved to the U.K. from the Caribbean (in his case the island of Nevis) in search of a better life. At that time, West Indian communities were springing up around the country; Martin Brown settled in Leeds, which contained one of the largest of these communities, and found work at a local engineering company.

In time he met Andrea, a white girl, and they married. At the time, interracial weddings weren't particularly common, and the Browns had to deal with a number of people who opposed their union.

Love being love, they weren't about to let something as minor as skin color stop them, and a few years later, a daughter, Melanie, arrived on the scene.

Having a mixed racial background caused Mel B some confusion when she was a little kid. "My surname's Brown," she said, "and I thought when I was really young that I was called Brown because I *am* brown. I wasn't black and I wasn't white. And I couldn't understand why so-and-so wasn't called White...."

Melanie grew up smart and surprisingly strong, even if she did need glasses, which she still wears. "I only played with boys," she said of her childhood. "Girls were always crybabies."

As she grew into adolescence, her interests leaned toward the arts, and her parents allowed her to take acting and ballet lessons. But that wasn't enough for her. A few hours after school didn't satisfy the hunger she felt to perform. And so she applied to the Intake School of Performing Arts in Leeds, and passed the audition to become a student.

At first it seemed that dance was her real talent, and by the time she was a teenager, she been accepted as a pupil at the prestigious Northern School of Dance, no small achievement. But Mel wasn't about to let herself be limited to one thing. Once she was old enough, she enrolled at Leeds College of Music to study voice and percussion. Although she never did quite manage to master the drums, every little bit of training was useful.

Studious as she was, Mel also had a wild streak that

would rear its head once in a while. "I've always been the black sheep in my family," she admitted later with a laugh.

She could be loud, raucous, and unruly. But then, at other times, she would become remarkably quiet and contemplative, thinking through the issues that most teenagers confront: Why am I here? What am I going to do? Is there a point to life?

School had plenty of good points, but as interesting as it was, it wasn't getting her paid work. The only answer was to leave and start pounding the pavement, attending auditions and putting in applications. She tried out for the part of Fion on the top British soap opera *Coronation Street*, but didn't make the grade, losing out to another Leeds girl and having to content herself with a couple of walk-on parts and an appearance in a shoe commercial.

And she even tried her hand at the beauty pageants, entering the Leeds Miss Caribbean Sun contest. She seemed a shoo-in to win, but ended up with second prize.

It wasn't turning out the way she'd planned, but Mel B wasn't about to give up. She continued practicing her dancing and took voice coaching during the day, leaving the evenings free to attend auditions.

After a while, though, she *really* needed to earn some money. There was one easy answer—to get a job dancing in one of the men's clubs in town, to become a "private dancer" in a nightclub.

The one that took her on was called Yell, located in a side street in Leeds city center. It was raunchy, but not as bad as some people have claimed. There was no nudity; in fact, Mel didn't even have to dance topless. As long as she wore a scanty bikini, everyone was happy.

By that time she had a steady boyfriend, and quite a

catch he was! Steve Mulrain was twenty, three years older than Mel, and an apprentice soccer player with Leeds United, the team Mel had supported since she was a baby. They'd met while they were both out clubbing—Mel's favorite way to spend an evening. He'd had no choice but to notice her.

"That night she looked sensational," he recalled. "She had on a short, tight silver dress with black knee-high boots."

While she wasn't paying attention to Steve at first, he was persistent, and by the end of the evening she'd agreed to go out with him, partly because she had a weakness for soccer players.

"I'm kind of into [soccer] but in a girlie way," she said. "I like looking at their legs and the way they get all sweaty."

When she began dancing at Yell, Mel was quite nervous, not sure what she'd let herself in for. "It's quite funny looking at her now," said Lisa Adamczyk, who was her boss at the club, "because in the old days she wouldn't say boo to a goose. She was a sweet, quiet girl who wanted to get on."

Once she had grown used to the routine, and the money she could earn without having to take all her clothes off, Mel loosened up a bit. "She'd come across as the wildest girl you'd ever meet, but underneath was a hardworking girl who was faithful to her boyfriend," Adamczyk remembered.

Mel received no shortage of offers from the men who came around, but it was Steve she wanted to be with. "They were inseparable," Adamczyk continued, "but that was why Mel was so special."

The work kept her fit, and the money helped her buy clothes, but dancing at Yell also left her hungry. With all the energy she expended every night—and when she wasn't dancing at the club, she'd be out with Steve or her friends, making the rounds of the other dance clubs in Leeds—a salad just wasn't enough. She ate fish and chips (her favorite food), Chinese, Italian, curries, everything. "Mel didn't care what she ate," Steve said. "She had a huge appetite!"

Despite her voraciousness she managed never to put

on any weight, remaining lean and occasionally mean.

Mel was coming to realize that her life in Leeds was at a dead end. If she really wanted to get famous, she was going to have to move to London, the center of the British entertainment industry. Working at Yell brought in good money, but it wasn't going to help her become a star.

She was left with a choice—to stay with Steve or head south on her own. It was her life, and she had to live it. There was only one solution: go to London.

Nothing happened magically when she arrived. Fortune wasn't waiting for her at the gates to the city. Like the other girls who'd end up "Spicy," she took whatever jobs she could find to pay the rent and feed herself.

"I did telesales [telemarketing] for a newspaper and a few tacky pantomimes." But there was no return to "private" dancing; she'd had more than enough of that.

One thing she did love about London was the variety of its club scene. There were so many to choose among, offering every imaginable type of music to dance to. It was the way she loved to spend a night, often well into the early hours of the morning, just dancing, dancing, dancing. If it was good hip-hop or jungle, so much the better. And it's something she still loves to do, although her time to go clubbing has become more limited these days—she's just too busy.

"I haven't had that much chance recently for all that," she admitted, "so I hope all the girls out there are getting out and about. I mean, all that gets you noticed by the men!"

Still, when she does manage a free evening these days, she makes sure she enjoys herself. All the way. "She's the best person to go partying with," Emma said. "She won't just go to one club, she'll go to all of them."

In the clubs, she could be a real extrovert, loud, obnoxious, and nobody cared. Everyone was there for the sounds and a good time.

The clubs were fun, but going to them meant spending money, not earning it. In between jobs, Mel was kept busy making the rounds of auditions, checking all the magazines every week to learn about the showbiz opportunities. She didn't, as has been suggested, once share an apartment with Mel C (although they did share a room at the house in Maidenhead); in fact, they never met until they were both chosen to become part of an unnamed new band.

With her strong, assertive personality, it was quite natural that Mel B would make herself heard among the girls. She can be honest—brutally so at times—and doesn't mince words. During those early months with the other girls, she was in everyone's face, and really didn't care. She wanted success, and expected everyone else to want it just as badly.

Inevitably, she and Geri butted heads a few times.

They both know how to stand up for themselves, and both can be domineering and bossy. Once they worked out their problems, though, the Spice Girls found themselves with two leaders who were working together.

"Me and Geri lay down the law," Mel said. "I do the brutal attack while Geri is fair and listens to both sides of the story."

For all that she can be totally wild and utterly crazy, there's still a tender side to Mel B. When the Girls hit it big, the first thing she did was to go out and buy her mother a new car, a sporty Volkswagen Cabriolet. Mel would love to support Andrea, but her mother insists on keeping her job as a cleaner in a Leeds department store. When the Spices took a break, Mel traveled to the West Indies to see her father's homeland for the first time and meet her grandmother, although the woman didn't quite know what to make of this wild grandchild as she strode around yelling, "Girl Power!" As Mel pointed out, "They don't know about the Spice Girls yet," which must mean the islands are among the few places on the planet that don't. But they will, they're bound to soon enough....

Initially, Mel's mother, Andrea Brown, was very skeptical about her daughter becoming a Spice girl, thinking it would be like so many other best-laid plans and end up going nowhere. Now, though, she's immensely proud of Mel and the two have become closer than ever.

"I could see she had talent and she's always been determined to do well."

Once Emma joined the band, Mel knew that something just clicked, a perfect kind of chemistry had come together that set the girls apart. They were all striving for the same thing. It worked, she said, because "we're five individuals; we all dress differently

but we've got real spirit and camaraderie that you only get between girls."

And they certainly were all very individual. Each had her specific look, and for Mel B, it was that of street fashion. Combat pants, cool crop tops, vests, big boots, and big hair ("Every band needs big hair"). They were the kind of clothes you'd wear to go clubbing or raving, functional, easily available, in layers you could take off as you grew sweaty from dancing. If she wanted to dress up—something she enjoys—there were hot pants and long fake-fur coats.

That distinguished her well enough, but she decided to take it two steps further. First of all, she had her stomach tattooed with a Japanese symbol meaning "Spirit, Heart, and Mind." Then, not to be outdone by Mel C's pierced nose, or Geri's pierced belly button, she went all the way and had her tongue pierced! Arriving back at the house in Maidenhead, she wanted to be able to feel this change properly, so she insisted that all the others scrog (neck) with her.

These days it's become one of her most apparent features (especially when she sticks her tongue out at guys), even if it has caused her to lisp a bit. But there's no doubting that it's hip, or that, with their various tattoos and piercings, the Spices aren't merely faking it. They're very, very real.

When Mel B left Leeds, she left Steve behind. But there have, inevitably, been more than a few boys in her life since then. In Maidenhead, she dated Mark Brownsmith for a while. But for the last couple of years, it's a guy referred to mysteriously as just Richard who's been the love in her life. He's an engraver; beyond saying this, she's kept her romantic life very private, although she insists, "Some of us have boyfriends, but men don't rule our lives. They should be like mates and should never try to come between you and your mates."

At the moment, Mel and Richard live together in London. Late in 1996, a fire destroyed their flat, taking with it all Mel's prized possessions—the gold and platinum records, furniture, photos, everything.

Whereas Geri's the erudite one in the band, willing and able to talk about anything and everything, Mel B likes to make her points quickly and loudly. She can be the rowdiest and raunchiest of the lot—quite a feat, really, when you consider that they all insist on being heard.

And even more than the others, Mel is always up for a laugh. There's nothing and no one going to put her in her place; it doesn't matter who you are. Which makes her a very useful friend to have around, as Emma pointed out: "If you get into an awkward situation with a boy, she'll rescue you by pointing at him and shouting, 'No!'"

Even big-screen hunks don't leave her in awe. When the Girls were at a party in Los Angeles, Mel B spotted Brad Pitt across the room. Most women would have been in awe, just stopping to stare, afraid to get near him, let alone say anything. Not Mel. She walked up, slapped him on the back, nodded, and said, "All right, Brad?"

But that's the kind of action that's typical of her; as she herself put it, "You can get away with anything as long as you're cheeky." She once said, "Be happy with yourself and the rest is a doddle"—a breeze, we'd say in the States—and that's exactly the way she chooses to live her life. It's a funky, fresh attitude, and she makes sure it carries over into her work.

"We're revitalizing pop," she said of the Spices. "Our songs are pop with intelligence and personality, unlike some! None of our songs are about wishy-washy love...."

And it's true. It's pop, but with an edge, a lot of which comes from Mel's raps, her background in hip-hop and love of phat beats. Of all the Spices, she's the one who's really down with the club scene, who knows exactly what's going on in music. And she's determined to see that reflected in the Spice tunes.

With Tina Turner as a role model and hero, Mel knows there's very little she can't achieve (after all, who else at fifty-seven looks as good, or shows as much leg, as Tina?) if she puts her mind to it and really works. In spite of the tremendous record sales and reception the Spices have already achieved, she knows they've only just begun to explore the possibilities.

As Victoria said, "Mel B is the ultimate Spice girl—pretty, clever, crazy, and impudent. Sometimes I would like to be like she is."

And if the boys are scared of Scary Spice (in the *Sky International* poll she could only manage fourth place, with 9.2 percent of the vote), then that's their problem, not hers. She's proud and loud, and she's going to tell you exactly what she's thinking. If you can't deal with it, better get out of her way. Now.

CHAPTER ELEVEN

GIRL POWER NOW!

Okay, so the Spices keep talking about Girl Power. But is it really something they believe, or just a very careful, very cynical marketing ploy? And if it is for real, then just what is it all about?

Feminism isn't exactly new. Once women finally got the vote, in the twentieth century—and they had to fight and yell a long time for that—their search for a better life moved on to other issues—like equal rights, equal pay. Once women's studies started being taught in colleges, though, the movement became bogged down in academic theory. Most everyone (at least, most women) agreed that feminism was a good thing. But deciding exactly what feminism was, was much harder.

But then there was a new generation that didn't want to spend all its time discussing things. They'd seen that talk didn't achieve results; the arguments went round and round in circles, and the guys still kept control. If they were really going to make some changes, the girls needed to take things into their own hands, to act instead of talk.

And so Girl Power was born.

It wasn't about any one issue, just a feeling that females had taken enough garbage, and they weren't about to take any more. The girls had declared their independence.

For far too long, it had been men calling all the shots. Girl Power wasn't standing for that. Girls were going their own way, doing exactly what they wanted, with whomever they wanted, whenever they wanted.

In the past, if a girl had a boyfriend, he was the center of her world. No more of that! Romances come and go, but it's your friends who stick around, and it's important not to ignore them. If your boyfriend can't get along with your friends, then it's definitely time to think about dumping him (which is, really, the message of "Wannabe").

If you want to dress tough, that's cool. It's the nineties—anything goes in terms of fashion. Retro, classy, hip. The important thing is to be yourself at all times, to be proud of being a girl, rather than being made to feel like a second-class citizen because of your sex. Whatever way you want to look, it's time to go for it. If people criticize you, that's their problem, not yours. If you're happy, why care what anyone else thinks? Clothes have always been a form of self-expression. You don't need to follow the herd and pick up on every trend anymore. It's much more important to be comfortable and be yourself.

"Girl Power is about doing exactly what you want to do, not pleasing others," Geri said.

Being meek and mild might get you awards for good behavior, but it won't get you what you want in life.

The men have been so used to having it their way and never having to listen to women that girls have to shout themselves hoarse in order to be heard in the world. So if that's what you need to do to make some changes, then don't be afraid of doing it. The guys might not like it, but so what? Get in their faces and make sure they understand what you're saying. If they think no means yes, do whatever you have to do to get your point across. Be forceful if you have to. After all, wimps never go anywhere, do they?

The same thing applies to getting what you really, really want. There's only one way to achieve your goals, and that's to get in there and fight like crazy to succeed. Give it all you've got. No one's going to hand you your life on a plate. You have to figure out what you want and pursue it relentlessly. The incredibly positive part of Girl Power is that it believes there's nothing you can't achieve if you try hard enough and really work for it. Maybe success won't end up being quite the thing you at first thought you needed, but it'll be something good, and you'll have grown as a person along the way. But you have to have confidence in yourself. Don't let anyone tell you that you can never do something because you're female. That's the old way. It's out of here.

"We're turning the tables on the guys," Emma said. "But we think that's equality."

It's all about standing up for yourself, but Girl Power has nothing to do with any of the old feminist ideas about hating men. Quite the opposite. These days there's nothing wrong with a girl looking drop-dead sexy if that's what she wants. And she can flirt, be outrageous around the boys, if that's the way she wishes to be. *That's* turning the tables. *They've* been doing it for so long, and thinking how clever they were—when the girls give them a taste of their own medicine, see how they like it. Boys might be great, but they're not God's gift (even if many of them seem to think they are).

If a girl sees a cute guy she likes, she's not going to get him by waiting around and hoping he'll notice her. You have to be assertive and go for what you want. If you want a guy, sitting at home and hoping for one won't do any good at all.

"You have to get yourself out and about to get noticed by the men," Mel B advised. "Take a leaf out of my book; if you fancy him—tell him. If you want him, get him—do it with chick style and boldness. Say, 'I fancy you, I do.' It's a killer. What have you got to lose—nothin'."

It's great advice. And once you've got him, don't

ever let him boss you around. If he tries, put him very firmly in his place. And if that doesn't work, it's time to say good-bye. And be up-front about that, too. Don't just forget to call him back. Let him know what he's done wrong—maybe he'll even learn something.

"When dumping a bloke, be straight and direct," Geri has said. "Don't beat around the bush. Just say, 'See ya, wouldn't want to be ya!'"

And should he have the gall to try to hit on one of your friends when he's dating you, that's it. It's the end of the road right there.

"If my best friend's boyfriend came on to me I'd tell him where to get off," Mel C said firmly. "Friends are far more important. It's one of those unwritten laws— thou shall not snog"—neck with—"your friend's bloke."

Above all, Girl Power demands that you approach life with attitude. With confidence and assurance. Be cheeky, don't let anyone put you down. Don't let life happen to you—it's far too important for that. Make your own decisions, your own changes. Be in control of your own destiny, your own life. And don't set your sights too low. If it takes a little sass to get things moving your way, then use it. You're a person, with so much at your command. You can't be afraid of things. You're a girl, you're strong, you're powerful, you can make things happen for yourself. No one's better than you, and don't let anyone tell you they are; it doesn't matter whether they have money, position, wealth, or whatever. Support your girl friends, and let them support you, too. Don't place all your hopes on a guy. He might be great, but more than anything you have to rely on yourself, and be happy with yourself, first.

And that, in a nutshell, is what Girl Power is all about. It seems pretty obvious, really, but the way the world has been, it ends up sounding quite revolutionary. Are men really ready for strong women? No one really knows for sure, but they're about to find out, since the Girl Power revolution is finally under way.

But is the Spice take on Girl Power anything more than a blatant marketing ploy to attract a female audience? Do they really believe it, or is it simply another set of words to spout?

Well, if actions really do speak louder than words, then the Spice Girls are screaming Girl Power. They're sassy, they're loud, they're rude, they're everything "polite," conventional girls should never be. They say everything that's on their minds, no matter who's listening.

One thing they're not going to take is being treated like bimbos.

They're Girl Power in Technicolor and 3-D. Proof that you can look like a babe, be tough, and still have a sweet center. Proof that hard work and determination really can get you the things you want.

If it had all been some cunning marketing ploy, it would have worn off long ago, once the Girls had become megastars and didn't need it anymore. But

Girl Power remains very much a part of the Spicy phi-losophy of life, maybe even its very heart. The Girls haven't ditched Girl Power, and they never will. And that's because they understand how important it is—not only to them, but to every female.

As pop stars, they have a better chance of spreading the message than any politician or feminist academic. Most people would rather hear a pop song than a speech. And the girls who are dancing to "Wannabe" today, and taking in what it has to say, are the leaders of tomorrow. Perhaps it's a hokey thing to say about a pop group these days, but the Spices really could change the world.

And why not? It's happened to other groups who didn't even set out to say anything. The Spices arrived with that rarest of things for an all-female pop group—an agenda. They were about more than suc-cess, as the Girl Power sticker or the slogans on the booklet of their album made clear. Shouting *was* fun, and it really could become a girl's world. At least, it could be if the Spices had anything to do with it.

You could call them the poster girls for Girl Power.

They're real and totally committed to the cause. Just so long as it's understood that they're going to have fun while they do it. But in any interview you read with any of the Girls, the topic comes up—and usually it's them who are raising it. Geri, in particular, is the one who'll talk about it—but then she'll gladly talk about anything, at any time, to anyone—the one who seems most involved. Yet the others are also whole-hearted supporters of Girl Power. It's become a major part of their lives.

From their own experiences, they all know perfectly well what it's like to be controlled by men. And they've learned that with solidarity, banding together, they can make things happen. They have strength individually, but as a group they're completely unstoppable. They learned the hard way that the most important people in your life are your girl friends. Even though Emma, Mel B, and Victoria all have boyfriends, they know that the girls are the ones who'll always be there for them when the boys have all gone. They don't just sing about it, they put it into action.

They *live* Girl Power every day. They're sassy, abrasive, and frequently outrageous. They outplay the guys at every turn. But that's what it's all about. That's what they *have* to do. And all the while they remain perfectly, totally female. Makeup, heels, hose, as sexy as you please, they're the male dream and the male nightmare all rolled into five lovely packages.

They're role models for the girls of today. If just a tenth of the girls who buy their records take the idea of Girl Power to heart, the world will become a very different place in a few years. And that can only be a huge improvement. After all the political bantering, the speeches and demonstrations, wouldn't it be a great irony if the people who made the biggest leap for women were a pop group?

Geri's often said that it's more important for her to make a difference in one girl's life than to have all the success she's enjoyed so far. Well, there seems to be a very good chance that she'll do both. In Britain, there are already seven-year-olds who are listening.

The message is being heard loud and clear by the media as well. In November 1996, *The Independent*, one of the most prestigious and respected newspapers in England, ran a long article about Girl Power and the impact the Spices could have on British society. Apart from being another indication of how much they've become part of Britain's social fabric, it meant that they were finally being taken seriously, that someone was willing to believe that Girl Power was a very real thing to them, and not just a strategy to sell more records. They really were becoming a force for change in society.

So yes, the Spices do believe everything they say. And Girl Power is here, now. It's no longer the wave of the future; better catch the surf today.

CHAPTER TWELVE

SAY YOU'LL BE THERE

nce "Wannabe" slipped from the number one position, the big question was whether or not the Spices could repeat its success. Hitting the top first time out was remarkable enough. Twice in succession would have been utterly incredible.

People didn't have to wait too long to find out. Even before "Say You'll Be There" reached the stores, it was a massive, surefire hit. The week before its late-September release, advance orders topped 334,000—the highest Virgin had ever recorded for a single. Every copy from that order, and even more—bringing it up to a total of 350,000—zoomed out of the stores in the first week.

It rocketed straight into the chart at number one, toppling Boyzone in a wonderful "girl band beats boy band" scenario. A week later "Say You'll Be There" went platinum. Anyone who doubted that the Spices were the biggest thing to hit music in years suddenly found himself eating his words.

Naturally, the Girls had shot a video to accompany the song. It was filmed in the California desert, not far from Los Angeles, and its style paid homage to all manner of sixties flash and trash. There were shades of *The Avengers*, that cult TV show that had brought fame to Diana Rigg (and later, Joanna Lumley, who'd become a camp icon as Patsy in the British TV show *Absolutely Fabulous*), 007, even the awful Russ Meyer girlie movies.

But it was quite definitely a Girl Power video, with the Spices showing the guys just how superior women could be with some very elaborately choreographed karate moves (taught to the others, of course, by Goju blue-belt Emma) and dancing, and the final ignominy for a male—being blindfolded by a black bra! It was fun, it made its point, and it also managed to have a wonderfully glamorous edge.

A video was a standard industry way to sell a single, but by now it was debatable whether the Spices even needed one. A few still pictures to accompany the song would probably have done the trick just as well for most of the population. In a few short months, the Spices had become *that* big.

"Say You'll Be There" was a romantic jam in the best tradition, a mid-paced R&B groove with a funky keyboard line that gave all the Girls a chance to show off their singing voices. It didn't have the up-tempo hooks of "Wannabe," but this was meant to be something different, a little softer, music to play as the night was starting to wind down, to dance slow or get close to someone. And with two other mixes of the song available on the single, you could get it almost any way you wanted it.

Smooth as it was, there was certainly nothing ditsy about the lyrics. Once again, it was definitely on the Girl Power trip. This wasn't about a girl falling hopelessly for a boy and trying to make him love her, but the other way around. Turnabout is fair play, after all. And although the Spices had originally decided that being platonic friends was best, they were willing to give "him" a try, and would even give it their all—but there was a condition attached. He had to promise to be there for her. And that didn't mean just being there when it suited him, but always, especially when they needed him.

Maybe it didn't seem to be, but in its own way the song was groundbreaking. Women rarely mixed interpersonal romance and personal strength in their music. They were always the ones chasing and sighing over the boys. But music never had the Spice Girls to contend with before. They'd announced their intentions in "Wannabe," and now they were following through on them.

This time, however, they couldn't sustain another

seven weeks at number one. After two weeks at the top, they were forced to cede the crown to Robson and Jerome's remake of "What Becomes of the Broken Hearted?"

By then the chart position of the song almost didn't matter. Even though they'd released only two singles, no one in pop music had had a bigger year. And considering it was still only October, who could say what they were likely to achieve before it was all over.

"We're not trying to trip the guys up," Emma insisted. "We just hope to pave the way for girl bands, to encourage girls to get together and make music that feels good."

Still, they never expected all of this to happen. No one, even in their craziest fantasies, could have imagined how big the Spices had become, as Victoria acknowledged. "Sometimes you just can't quite believe it," she said. "The support has been unbelievable! We're living our wildest dreams!"

Certainly the pop life was being very good to them. But it showed what could happen if you were willing to give it everything, take your best shot, and push to win.

"Say You'll Be There" did raise a small stir of controversy. It was at the top of the charts in England, and heading that way in a number of other countries around the world, when the Spices found themselves served with a law suit for plagiarism.

Idit Schectman, a nineteen-year-old Sabra girl serving in the Israeli armed forces, claimed that the melody of "Say You'll Be There" had been lifted from her song "Come to Me."

As their success exploded to new heights, everyone seemed to want a piece of the Spices. They were on television shows. They cut short a promotional tour to rush back to England and draw the numbers for the first Wednesday national lottery, called Winsday. For five girls who'd only very recently become pop stars, they'd quickly turned into what could only be called national icons. Comedians made jokes about them and *everyone understood*. They were that big.

Big almost everywhere, that is. One place hadn't been exposed to the Spice vibe yet, and that was America. The group had been there to film the video for "Say You'll Be There," but neither of their singles had yet been released. It seemed ridiculous, given that the Girls had already conquered every other major market in the world. What were they waiting for?

Well, there was a method to the madness (and, according to Geri, madness was fine as long as there really was a method behind it), as Phil Quartararo, president of Virgin Records America explained to *The New York Times*. The company was waiting, he said, until hip-hop and alternative music began to fade out of the charts, leaving an open field for the pure pop of the Spices.

It all made good sense, actually, even though it meant that America seriously lagged behind the rest of the globe. Unlike most countries, America has no national radio stations. It doesn't even have a television chart show that is seen in every market. While a buzz was slowly building as people began to hear about the Spices from friends in Europe and Asia, it would take a while before America would be ready for the Spice Revolution. You could say that the Girls were holding their fire until they saw the whites of America's eyes.

And there were more immediate concerns at home. At the beginning of November, just in time to be on everyone's Christmas list, the album *Spice* was released. It was probably the most anticipated record of the year.

Even before it hit the stores, it had gone silver, with sixty thousand advance copies ordered. While it was up against the usual seasonal fare—the "Best Ofs" and new releases by established, often major artists, in 1996 there was just no competition. *Spice* very handily cruised to the head of the album charts on the day of its release and unpacked its bags, so to speak, preparing to stay ensconced there for quite a while. Even George Michael, whose new album had been so eagerly awaited, didn't have a chance against the Girl squad.

"It's all happening so fast," Mel B said about the

whirlwind. "One day we were no one, the next we were beating George Michael to number one."

But the days of being nobodies were far behind them now. The sales of the singles had been exceptional, but *Spice* was vanishing from stores as quickly as the clerks could put it on the racks. By the end of January 1997, it would have gone platinum six times over (in the U.K., 300,000 units sold equals a platinum record), with a total of 1.8 million copies sold.

The culmination of many hours of studio work, *Spice* was as close to modern pop perfection as anyone had ever come. There simply wasn't a bad song among the ten on the record. There wasn't even any of the usual "filler," lower-quality material that bands use to pad out their albums. Both the singles were there; indeed, they were the leadoff tracks. But virtually every song could have stood as a single (and all would almost certainly have been hits).

The third track, "2 Become 1," had, in fact, already been earmarked as the next single, to be released just before Christmas. Then came "Love Thing," which started with a strong, extremely funky seventies groove, with plenty of soulful harmonies—once more the Girls did their trademark freestyling of lyrics, both singing and in the rap—and added a nineties sheen to the production. The bass took deep bounces, propelling the tune. Up-tempo as the song was, it was impossible to resist. And it continued strongly in the

Girl Power lyrical tradition. These girls weren't about to let themselves be pushovers for any boy. They were more powerful than that. If "he" wanted them, he needed to prove himself. The Girls weren't just out there waiting for the first guy to come along—he had to measure up, and if he tried to come between one of the Spices and her "sistahs," then he might as well just get out of the way, because they weren't standing still for that.

"Last Time Lover" mined a vein in the hip-hop mother lode, with a heavy beat and a little turntable scratching, topped off by some very sexy singing, as befitted one of the Girls talking to a guy she was interested in. But he'd better know that he had to play it her way. No rush, let it develop naturally. If it was love, she still wasn't about to let herself be overwhelmed, because she was very choosy about who she dated. It was sultry, it was cool, and it was very sexy, a slithering bass line sliding the song along.

Of course it continued the Girl Power theme; that was what propelled the whole album. It was about looking good, going for what you wanted, and making sure you said no if it all seemed to be moving too fast. Strong stuff for pop music, but a very positive message to be putting across, certainly to girls, but also to boys, perhaps the ones who need to hear it the most. If Girl Power ever required a manifesto, *Spice* really seemed to be providing it. There was nothing halfhearted or coy about these lyrics; even an older generation of feminists could have been proud of them.

Every pop album needs at least one sweet ballad, though, and that was what the Spices served up next. But "Mama" wasn't a little saccharine weepie. It might have started with a soft acoustic guitar figure, but some scratching and hip-hop drums took the soppy edge off the music. It made a very pleasant change to have a song like this sung to someone's mother instead of boyfriend, though, and it was hard to deny the sentiments. A lot of people really do have good relationships with their mothers—at least, once their teenage years are over. Also impressive was the arrangement, which used a string section to swell the voices, and then, toward the end, brought in a gospel choir. At five minutes and three seconds, it was easily the longest track on the record, but it needed that "epic" feel to fully make its point.

The next track was a definite shift in gears. "Who Do You Think You Are?" borrowed its feel very heavily from the pages of seventies funk, disco, and pop music, so much so that it wouldn't have seemed out of place on the charts for 1975. Wonderful, cascading harmonies led the chorus (just in case people didn't think the girls could manage harmony), while the verse bombed along on a very slinky groove that seemed to make musical references to most of the soul bands of two decades ago. And there was absolutely nothing wrong with that. Retro was cool, particularly in soul and disco, and that phat driving, rising, popped bass line knew it. Lyrically, it wasn't as strong as the rest of the record, but it could easily have served as a cautionary lesson to the Girls themselves. When they'd recorded it, in 1995, they couldn't have known just how huge they'd become, and this song was a piece of advice to a friend to keep her (or his) feet on the ground and not let success go to her head. From the way they acted, it seemed as if they'd taken the time to listen to the words themselves, luckily.

It was no surprise that "Something Kinda Funny" had been the song that convinced Virgin to sign the Spice Girls—it was one of the best, and musically one of the strongest, on the record. There were powerful echoes of the young Stevie Wonder (from around the time of the brilliant *Music of My Mind* and *Talking Book* albums) in the song's melody and arrangement, but with a real freshness—not just looking back and copying a style but reinventing it at the same time. This song had the *feel* of a real soul tune, and the Girls sang it exactly that way. After "Mama" and "Who Do You Think You Are?" the lyrics returned to Girl Power territory, offering very hopeful messages about enjoying the journey through life, and also warning boys that if they tried to dictate the game to the Spices, they'd end up left way behind. It had been an important song in the Girls' development, the first in which they really caught fire as an ensemble, and it was easy to understand why. Their voices clicked perfectly on it, locked together and woven around each other, first one up front, then another. The words had strength, the performance had real feeling and soul.

Beginning with its title, "Naked" made no secret of its intentions. At least, that was the way it seemed on the surface. And anyone could have been forgiven for thinking the song was purely about sex, specifically about losing one's virginity. Certainly, the slow jam had a very slinky, sexy groove, the kind of thing that was almost custom-made for loving. But the truth was that much more was going on inside. Yes, it was about making love for the first time—and from a girl's point of view, not a man's, which made for a very pleasant change—and all the anticipation and fear that goes along with this experience. Far more than that, though, it was about feminine strength, about making choices, whether to be with someone or to leave them if they treated you badly, as shown in the middle "phone call" section of the song. And it was also, implicitly, about being able to say no, and not allowing yourself to be pressured into something you aren't ready for. The Girls, naturally, are very aware of the power of their messages, and think long and hard before putting pen to paper for their lyrics. There was nothing on *Spice* that would ever show girls in anything less than full control of their own lives.

With the seriousness aside, it was time to finish the album with a slamming fast track, to go out on a very high note, and "If U Can't Dance" was the perfect choice for that. It sampled the groove of Digital Underground's "Humpty Dance" (which Digital Underground had taken from funksters Parliament/Funkadelic in the first place), and built a great dance track around it, one that showed just how real the Girls' club credentials actually were. A little touch of techno, a heavy helping of hip-hop, even a tribute to the early house scene of the Balearic Islands with a Spanish verse (no wonder the Spices were so big in Madrid!), it was a song that had all the power, pop smarts, and hooks of "Wannabe," making it an ideal concluding "bookend."

Inevitably, the track was a strong girl song, but one that approached politics with a sense of humor, from the viewpoint of a babe who loves to dance but only seems able to attract the nerds, not the hunks, when she's on the floor (an experience everyone has had at some point). She can dance, but they can't, and she's definitely not interested in anyone who can't move to the beat. It added a lighthearted touch to the disc, letting us know, just in case there was any doubt, that the Spices had a very well-developed sense of humor, and didn't take themselves *too* seriously. It also showed that you could be an advocate of Girl Power and still have a *very* good time.

And that was *Spice*. Did it fulfill all the expectations that had surrounded it? The answer was a resounding yes. The public answered with their wallets, sending it directly to number one. No one could deny the Spice Power anymore. Even the critics enjoyed it—not only those who wrote for the popular daily press, which had virtually become a Spice industry over the last few months, but the real music critics who wouldn't ordinarily look at a record that didn't have suitable alternative or dance credentials. The Spice Girls had achieved something very rare—they'd won over *everybody*. Even Britpop fans found themselves furtively lining up to buy the record, although they'd probably hide it in a dresser drawer and enjoy it when they were alone. The music and the vibe were infectious, and Britain had caught the disease. So did most of the rest of the world, with the album's pre-Christmas release in other parts of the globe producing the kind of business record-label executives usually only dream about.

A band like the Spice Girls comes along maybe once a generation. It may seem trite to compare them with The Beatles, since the Spices have yet to survive over the long haul, but in so many ways it's true. No other band since the Fab Four has had such an electrifying effect on the world. Sensational is an overused word, but in the case of the Girls, it's the right word.

And they just carried on being sensational. In the middle of November, the Girls ceremonially switched on the Christmas lights in London's Oxford Street, one of the world's great shopping thoroughfares. This was another confirmation of their enormous success. Such an invitation is normally given to *real* celebrities, true household names, not to the ragtags in music and show business. To ask a group of girls who just sang, and whose first record was only five months old, was remarkable. Britain had taken them to their hearts. The Girls had become every bit as English as fish and chips or a cuppa tea. They *were* England now, as much as the White Cliffs of Dover or Buckingham Palace. They'd certainly brought more money into Britain than most people. By now "Wannabe" had hit number one in thirty countries, and the names ran like a school geography lesson—Argentina, Australia, Belgium, Britain, the Czech Republic, Denmark, Estonia, Finland, Germany, Holland, Hong Kong, Ireland, Indonesia, Italy, Japan, Latvia, Lebanon, Malaysia, New Zealand, Norway, Portugal, Poland, South Africa, Spain, Switzerland, Sweden, and Thailand—a true cross section of the globe. The Spices really had taken on the world and brought it home.

Any appearance by the Spice Girls was certain to bring out the London crowds, and with the Christmas lighting event already an immensely popular holiday tradition, Oxford Street was jammed. The Spice mums were there, too, watching proudly as their daughters pulled the switch and the decorations lit up brightly.

But Jackie Addams noticed one face that wasn't smiling. A young child was jammed up against a barrier, rapidly being crushed by all the people pushing behind. Acting quickly, she was able to move the youngster to safety before the situation became life-threatening. So it wasn't only the Girls who made the papers the next morning, but a Spice mother, too.

Of course, the Spices didn't have universal approval; nobody ever can. There were those in Britain who seemed to think they needed to be put in their place, to be shown up as nothing more than bimbos. Perhaps such killjoys thought the Girls had undue influence over too many minds. Or perhaps they just resented the endless column inches of press being devoted to them. Whatever the reason, this undercurrent of feeling led to the most unusual request for an interview the group had received in their short career—a writer from *The Spectator* wanted to talk to them.

The Spectator wasn't a music paper. It wasn't a tabloid. It didn't even deal with popular culture. Its focus was politics. And it wanted to know where the Spice Girls stood politically.

The only political philosophy the Girls had espoused up to that point was Girl Power, hardly the type of doctrine to interest *The Spectator*'s readers. Faced with a barrage of questions on the issues and affairs of the day, they did their best to answer. Geri was proud to state that she thought former Prime Minister Margaret Thatcher was the first Spice Girl (although she dismissed current PM John Major as boring), and because of that, she came out adamantly on the side of the Conservative party, a position in which she was joined by Emma and Victoria. Mel C, a good Liverpudlian, remained a staunch Labour supporter (and she plans to lend her voice to this party in the upcoming British election), while Mel B had no time for any form of organized democracy; she preferred anarchy.

When the article was published, it naturally caught the eye of the tabloids, who were quick to jump on it. Even they had never thought of asking the Girls about politics, and they found it both strange and hilarious that anyone else would. Would the "Spice Vote" be a factor in the election? they wondered. Would the opinions of the Girls influence young voters?

The Spices themselves were far from happy with the way it all turned out. By their own admission, they didn't know a great deal about politics (they were far too busy to think of much but their own careers at the moment), but they felt that a good deal of what they had said had either been ignored or twisted to conform to a writer's agenda and place them in a bad light.

In the end, though, such tactics backfired. People

were supposed to laugh at the stupidity and gullibility of the Spices. Instead they found in their opinions more of themselves, people concerned with real lives as opposed to theories and doctrines, and shook their heads disapprovingly at *The Spectator* instead.

Once again, the Girls had come out on top.

release of a charity single was revealed, an cover of Bob Dylan's "Knockin' on Heaven's with an extra verse, the profits of which were the families and victims of the Dunblane cre, in which a rampaging gunman had killed ers and children in a Scottish elementary school. Vanting that record to do well, Virgin and the ices agreed to postpone their single's release until ust before Christmas, leaving, at least theoretically, the way open for the Dunblane record to be on top for the holiday. Although their intentions were good, however, the Spice Girls were simply *too* big. On the day of its release "2 Become 1" crashed right into the charts at number one.

Even when they didn't want it, it seemed, there was no denying them their place in the sun.

The song was issued in two versions. The "regular" version was the single, which was actually longer than the album track, followed by an orchestral take on "2 Become 1," then a new song, "One of These Girls," and the Junior Vasquez remix of "Wannabe."

Then there was the special Christmas pack, with a signed postcard and a different selection of tracks, all wrapped in cardboard, with spaces for "To..." and "From...," very handy as a last-minute stocking stuffer, especially for those who simply had to own everything Spicy. This version contained a remix of "2 Becomes 1" by Dave Way, and the Girls' version of the Christmas standard "Sleigh Ride."

Chapter · Thirt[een]

Christ[mas]
Presents

*W*ith two number-one sin[gles] number-one album, the Sp[ices] had already been a magic-carp[et] to the top of the world. But it wa[s] from over yet. December was just beginning, and th[e] Christmas season was going to bring the Girls plenty of presents to unwrap by the fire.

For example, a readers' poll in *Smash Hits*, the British pop magazine, netted them no fewer than three awards: Best British Act, Best New Act, and Best Video (for "Say You'll Be There"). *Top of the Pops*, the BBC television chart show, asked them to host its Christmas show, which was devoted to reprises of all the number-one hits of the year.

But the biggest gift of all would be their new single. "2 Become 1" had originally been scheduled for release in the middle of December, which would have assured it the prestigious Christmas top slot, given the way the Spices' popularity still continued to grow.

171

"2 Become 1" was very definitely a love song. Slow, dreamy, and sensuous, it was just made for pulling your partner close on the dance floor, or for celebrating a first-time experience of making love. Still, the Girls weren't going to write just an ordinary love song—if it was going to be sexy, there would have to be a very positive message involved, and there was. With its "Put it on" line, "2 Become 1" was also a safe-sex advertisement, one that might actually be listened to and obeyed. It was ultimately each person's decision whether to sleep with someone or not—and it should be a girl's decision, without any pressure or rush—but if she was determined to do it, she should remember to be careful and very, very safe. That way she'd avoid not only unwanted pregnanices, but also all sexually transmitted diseases, some of which could be deadly.

Such advice needed saying, and the song said it, in an understated and very gentle way. Without a doubt, safe sex was part of the Girl Power manifesto, and there was no way the Girls would not advocate it strongly.

"One of These Girls," the new song on the single, was an altogether different matter, though. Over a wonderful roller-coaster keyboard line, the Girls more or less told their own story. They were different, and they gloried in it. They were strong, and once they came together, nothing could stop them. It was a pounding Girl Power anthem, celebrating girls as indi-

·viduals, and even if it wasn't musically as strong as some of their other material, it was a worthwhile addition to the Spice Girls' catalog.

Their cover of "Sleigh Ride," though, was never meant to be taken seriously. Beginning with some conversation between them about the greater and lesser joys of Christmas before segueing into the melody, this recording was aimed strictly at the fans. It was a throwaway, really, but it was *fun*. The Girls didn't take it seriously or try to make it into a big production number. Instead they left it light and had a good laugh as they vamped their way through it.

The video for "2 Become 1" was an intriguing piece of work. At first glance it looked to have been filmed in New York, with the Girls moving at a normal pace while traffic flashed by them at something approaching hyperspeed. But that was just the director's trickery. It *was* New York in the background, all right, but the Spices hadn't been filmed there; they'd been in a studio and craftily superimposed over some time-lapse photography. That became quite apparent when Mel B began to walk the high wires of the Brooklyn Bridge—she was good, but not *that* good. It was clever, and the illusion it created was entertaining.

On Christmas Day, Britain got plenty of Spice with its festive meal when the Girls hosted an hour-long *Top of the Pops* special. They clowned, they laughed. They made fun of Chippendale hunks, wore Groucho

glasses and eyebrows, teased each other, dissed the guys. In other words, they were themselves in front of the cameras. And on top of that, they performed all three of their hits, reminding the nation just what a tremendous year they'd had. Victoria looked smooth in a short white dress, Geri over the top and trashy in a teddy and platform boots, Emma exuded sweetness and innocence in white and purple, Mel B looked outrageous in a leopardskin bikini, boots, and a fake-fur coat, while Mel C was her usual sportswearing self. A couple of years before, they'd warned people that they'd replace Take That, and the show saw Robbie Williams, the former heartthrob of that band, introducing his successors as pop heroes. But not pop kings this time. Pop *queens*.

"Our plan is to spice up the world big time," Geri had announced, and as the year wound to a close, it was obvious that they'd succeeded. And Mel B had obviously taken her own advice when she said, "What's the point of hanging around—go for it!"

But even in the last days of 1996, the surprises didn't stop coming. When the BRIT Award (the British version of the Grammys) nominations were announced, the Spice Girls found themselves listed in a remarkable five categories.

They were nominated twice for Best Video, both for "Wannabe" and "Say You'll Be There," and "Wannabe" was in the running for Best British Single, while the band appeared in both the Best Newcomer and Best British Group categories.

Considering how much they'd achieved, the five nominations might have seemed nothing more than justice, but they were actually quite unusual, since the BRIT nominating committee tends to steer well clear of pop music, preferring things a little more off the beaten commerical path (although with Oasis the year before, they'd had the best of both worlds). So it was a real testament to Spice Power that the Girls had conquered all those ingrained prejudices. But now they'd have to wait almost two months, until February 24, 1997, to learn if all those nominations would translate into any awards.

It had been a stupendous year, to say the very least. Back in January, at the time of the album's completion, none of the Girls could have envisioned how their lives would change in a mere twelve months. They'd done it...and done it, and done it again.

"Where I am now is proof if you want something badly enough you can get it," Mel C said, and it really seemed to be true. The Spices had invested so much time and energy into the band, and it had paid off in the biggest way possible.

Six months not only changed their lives beyond recognition, but also a country. Spicemania was spreading like wildfire in nations all over the world.

It was as if every dream Geri, Mel B, Mel C, Emma, and Victoria had ever dreamed had suddenly become real. In less than one hundred and eighty days they'd gone from nobodies to global celebrities. The history of pop music had never seen anything to match it, or even come close.

Perhaps the most amazing thing was that in all the whirlwind and hoopla of celebrity, the Girls managed to keep their heads and their senses of humor. It would have been so easy for their egos to have become inflated in their newfound status as pop royalty. By now they needed bodyguards, and secretaries to answer the stacks of fan mail (although the Girls tried hard to read the mail themselves, and Emma said, "If there's a couple that are specifically for me then I will definitely [read them]"). It was no longer possible to live a "real" life, what with the demands on their waking hours, plane trips across continents, public appearances, and rounds of interviews. But they managed it all with very good grace, a loud, bawdy sense of fun to overcome the endless hours of travel, and a deep sense of friendship between them that was just growing stronger and stronger every day.

Still, they needed a break. After achieving so much, so fast, it was time for a rest so they could get their heads straight. Particularly as the next test they faced in their quest to conquer the world could well be the toughest—breaking through in America. The North American continent hadn't been kind to British acts during the nineties. With the exception of Oasis, it had remained very insular, still enjoying its success in exporting the grungy Seattle sound to England. It had been many years since any out-and-out pop band from Britain had made an impact in the States. Would it be possible for the Spices to conquer America as they'd conquered the rest of the planet?

Time would tell, but they'd need all their energy and stamina if they were going to make it happen.

So a halt was called, and for a couple of weeks, each Girl went her separate way. Emma took her mother to Barbados. Mel C visited her father's homeland in the West Indies. Mel C took her mum and stepdad to the Middle East for the vacation of a lifetime and rode on a camel, while Geri and Emma sought the sun and the sand in other, quieter places.

Fit, tan, and ready for anything, in mid-January the Girls got back together, exchanging stories and jokes and preparing for what would either be the biggest thrill or the worst defeat of their lives. It was the Spice Girls versus America, and the only question was which one would come out on top.

CHAPTER FOURTEEN

SPICING UP AMERICA

*T*he only way to make America sit up and listen was with a publicity blitz. It had worked in Britain, and everyone believed it could work in the States. Given the size of the country, and the number of markets, the Girls had to travel a lot, and schmooze with and charm dozens of people. Los Angeles, New York, they had to go to so many places to reach out to the potential fans.

But was it even important to be big in America? With the rest of the world clamoring for them and following their every move, did they even need the U.S.?

Well, yes, they did. Not only was it the icing on the cake for any band, it was also the biggest single market for music in the world. Making it in America was truly making it. And for the Spices, "doing it," always means doing it all the way.

As Virgin president Phil Quartararo told *The New York Times*, "Success overseas usually doesn't mean much."

Actually it meant a lot—but not to Americans. They weren't that impressed by what kids in Manchester, or Tokyo, or Madrid were buying. America tended to look within itself. In the heartland, they liked what they liked and what they knew, and that was it. And those were the people the Spices had to reach.

"They may be a big story internationally," Quartararo continued, understanding his market, and his problem, "but the consumer in Amarillo or Peoria doesn't know what a Spice Girl is yet."

Neither did the consumers, it seemed, in Florida, where the Spices gave their first public performance, during a fair at the Hialeah racetrack outside Miami. It was a surprisingly low-key beginning to what would be a huge publicity campaign. Fewer than two thousand people watched as the Girls sang over prerecorded backing tracks and tried to get the crowd going by yelling, "Come on, Miami, do you want to see some Spicy action?"

It was hard work, but they eventually won that group over, if Jackie Rodrigues was a typical example. "I came for the fair," she said, "so the Spice Girls were a big bonus, they were cool."

But America was just too big to convert at the rate of two thousand fans at a time. Still, really, nobody knew who they were.

That, of course, would change very quickly. For the moment, though, the Girls began to spend time with radio programmers and disc jockeys, the people who would decide if "Wannabe" would even be played on the radio when it was released in a couple of weeks.

In the regions where advance copies had received radio play, the reaction had been massive. But it was *such* a strong song, so irresistible, that this was hardly surprising. Even so, there were those who believed the Spices were facing an impossible task. Strawberry Saroyan, writing in the British newspaper *Daily Express*, and displaying a profound bias toward No Doubt's excellent Gwen Steffani (who received several mentions in the article), felt that "They have no right to be pop stars; they're not only no better than us, they're just like us," as if being an ordinary girl and showing it was an automatic disqualification for stardom.

Wendy Jenson, the arts-and-entertainment editor for *Cosmopolitan*, aired other doubts. "There's a perception that the Spice Girls are a female New Kids on the Block," she said. "People who followed the New Kids remember soon after you bought those albums you never wanted to hear them again."

Spin contributing editor Jonathon Bernstein was similarly cynical, writing that, "I think it'll probably be over for them by Christmas."

Could these journalists be right? All around the world, millions of fans would beg to differ. And the bottom line always has to be the fans. Other journalists in the States had already taken opposing views, too, calling the Girls "the hottest Brit import since The

Beatles," and predicting that "they're going to be around for a long time to come." Just how long remained to be seen, but for now they were going from strength to strength—in America, just like everywhere else.

For the Girls, merely *being* in America was almost the best part of the Spice adventure so far. "I've always wanted to come to America ever since I was a baby," Emma said. By now she should have been used to foreign, exotic places, but she still found herself staring out of the limo windows all the way from the Los Angeles airport to their hotel. America has a magic hold on everyone from overseas.

But the Spices seemed to be quickly getting the same grip on America. "Outside radio stations and hotels they keep singing 'Wannabe' to us," Mel C said, laughing, "but in American accents. It's really funny. We always wanted to be an international act, not just big in the U.K. When we arrived in America we didn't think anyone would have a clue who we were. But people here seem to be catching on very fast."

And for Mel B, winning over the U.S. had become something of a mission. "We are fiercely patriotic. We feel we're out here doing it for Britain....We want to be successful the world over and we won't be happy until we are."

Another question to be asked was how would America react to Girl Power? After all, the country had been the home of the Riot Grrls—could the new idea spread into the mainstream? The Spices believed it could, partly because, as Emma noted, "It's not in-your-face feminism." And, Geri pointed out, "We think the average nineteen-year-old girl in Japan is not so different from the girl in Kentucky." Which was true; they both had to deal with very similar problems. But the Spices were going to show American girls there was more to it than that.

"We call it Girl Power but really, it's just having the confidence to make your dream come true," Geri explained. "Emma's a milkman's daughter and now she's one of the most famous faces around. Isn't that great?"

One thing that could definitely help the Spices' cause in America was MTV, which turned out to be solidly—if a little surprisingly—behind the Girls. To be fair, they'd long supported pop artists like Mariah Carey and Whitney Houston, but British pop groups hadn't been the most popular menu item on the video channel.

Maybe it was the energy of the "Wannabe" clip that won them over, or maybe it was the song itself, but whatever the reason, it was soon in heavy rotation on the station.

And, quite naturally, the Girls were big hits themselves everywhere they traveled on this publicity trip. Most Americans had always enjoyed—even if they hadn't always understood—the British sense of humor. And when it was five girls being funny and loud and somewhat risqué, then it was hard not to get caught up in the Spice spirit. Really, though, they were just being themselves.

"We're not afraid to speak our minds," Mel B said. "We don't mind saying something controversial...but fun! We want to spread the Spice vibe about."

And they were doing that in a big way, performing a cappella on the radio, posing for photographers. It was working; all the magazines were hungry for them. Even the writers who didn't care for the music, like Stephin Merritt (who sourly predicted they'd "scrabble for attention in the U.S.") in *Time Out New York*, ended up featuring them in articles. The Spice Girls were simply too big a story to ignore.

It was perhaps just as well that many journalists jumped on the Spice bandwagon so quickly. "Wannabe" was released on January 24, and leaped high into the *Billboard* singles chart, entering at number eleven, tying Alanis Morissette's record for the highest-ever debut entry. So even if *Entertainment Weekly* invoked ABBA and En Vogue in its review of the single, which it summed up as "goofily formulaic Euro pop," it was still important enough to cover, and the magazines wouldn't look quite so out of touch when the United States turned Spicy. *Sin* was much more succinct and accurate in its appraisal when it stated simply "should be huge."

Much to the delight of Victoria, since she claims it's the only magazine she reads, *Elle* gave the Girls a buzz.

America was falling very smartly into line with everyone else. Just one single out, heading for the top, the
press already eager to offer coverage—the magic carpet
was beginning to zoom in America.

By the time *Spice* was set for release, on February 4,
"Wannabe" was at number four, and looked poised to
climb all the way to the top. All the magazines and
newspapers were ready for this one, although some
weren't quite sure what to make of it. *People*, for example, noticed the obvious hip-hop influence (it would
have been difficult to miss, after all) but also saw some
reggae in there. Ultimately, to reviewer Amy Linden,
while the album wasn't "a work of great and mean-
ingful artistic importance, it sure is a lot of fun."

Then again, had the Girls wanted to make a heavy
artistic statement for the ages? Of course not. They
were, by their own admission, pop singers, and pop
music is meant to be of the moment. The really great
songs will hang around, but you can't aim for that. All
you can do—as the Spices had done—is write the best
material you can. The rest is up to history.

The *New York Post* brought up comparisons to The
Monkees, which were bound to appear sooner or later.
While the reviewer for this newspaper seemed to like
the Spices ("they're attractive, and deserve to knock
down lots of chips"), he was decidedly out of touch
with what was happening in the Spice World. Maybe
he thought it was hilarious to suggest that the Girls
get a TV show reminiscent of Mickey, Michael, Peter,

and Davy, but if he was so hip, how come he didn't know that the Spices had already signed to make their first movie, which would be in the style of *A Hard Day's Night* (the initial inspiration for the Monkees show, anyway), and which would be filmed in the summer of 1997?

In the *Los Angeles Times*, Sara Scribner wasn't any kinder. She, too, invoked the Monkees, and called the Girls "one-dimensional," which seemed to prove that she'd never met them. To her, "Wannabe" was little more than Neneh Cherry and Monie Love served up on a different plate, while the rest of *Spice* seemed strongly redolent of artists like Stevie Wonder, Lisa Stansfield, and Wham! "rehashed as bland sitcom pop."

It was a remarkably snotty attitude, as if something had to be second-rate just because it was pop music. In the previous five years so much dreck had been released under the heading of "alternative," but that label somehow seemed to confer instant credibility. There's nothing special in singing about your angst, particularly when so many so-called alternative bands do it so badly. That isn't art; it's trash. If the Spices were inspired by Stevie, by soul and hip-hop, why should these influences *diminish* their music?

The New York newspaper *Newsday* proved itself to be no better than the others, in this regard. Writer Tony Fletcher had obviously decided against the band from the word go. While he claimed to like a good pop song, "Wannabe" was not his idea of one, and he found the album "anything but fun to listen to," concluding that it was "awful." How ironic, then, that he should have interviewed Tom Poleman, the program director for Z100 (WHTZ), one of New York's biggest Top 40 stations, where every other request was for "Wannabe." To Poleman, "The Spice Girls represent having a good time and a fun attitude. Listeners have latched onto that. It's fun to listen to pop music again."

So who was out of step here? The critics, who thought they knew it all, or the public, the ones who called in requests and rushed to the record stores to spend their hard-earned cash on something they really, really wanted.

Fletcher, like the others, seemed to want to revere music as art, naming the ubiquitous Alanis, along with Fiona Apple, as "significantly more mature songwriters" than the Spices. But was even that true? Alanis might have wanted to be grown up, writing about angry phone calls to a former lover (an anger that reeked of self-pity), but the Spices advised girls to stand up for themselves, not to let themselves be used by men. Of the two, which was the more mature attitude? And if reviewers were going to condemn the Girls for their choice of influences, then what about Fiona Apple, whose music seemed directly inspired by Tori Amos?

The writers would hate to admit it, but there was

room for everybody in music, for Alanis and Fiona *and* the Spices. There wasn't even anything wrong with liking all three of them. They all had relevant messages. They could all be strong, in their own ways. The only difference was that the Spices made no pretense to being anything other than pop. And to a lot of writers, that had become a dirty word.

Not to Steve Volk, however. Writing in the *Philadelphia Inquirer*, he was one of the few who seemed to thoroughly enjoy *Spice*, even if he didn't find much originality in it. To him, the record was energetic and enthusiastic, and he summed it all up by saying there was "nothing wrong with having fun." At last! There was at least one member of the American press who was willing to accept the album on its own terms, instead of grudgingly admitting its existence or just complaining.

Meanwhile, *Entertainment Weekly* managed to find good points in the album. Ken Tucker called it "a devilishly good pop collection," and expressed his view that the Spices would survive and prosper beyond one-hit-wonder status, this despite the fact that "Wannabe" was still the standout track on the disc, "perky yet tough, catchy yet melodically surprising."

Despite these two favorable reviews, the majority of critics had little positive to say about the Spices. But not for the first time, though, the public was paying no attention whatsoever to the press, showing that the media's power to sway minds could be highly overrated. "Wannabe" was firmly lodged at number one and happily holding off all comers. And *Spice* had walked straight into the top ten of the *Billboard* album charts. The fans had spoken, and that was who the Girls cared about.

"They're the best people to meet," Geri said, "because they either tell us we're great or that we're rubbish."

And the fans definitely thought they were great.

Without a shot being fired, the Spice Girls had captured another continent. Granted, they weren't as big as they were in other countries and Americans couldn't tell Emma from Mel B, or Geri from Victoria. But this would come, all in good time. America was a very different nut to crack. The Spices had cracked the shell, but breaking it wide open might take awhile longer.

In the meantime, articles about the Girls were beginning to appear, and they really had become big news. *Spin*, *Entertainment Weekly*, *Bikini*, *The New York Times*, *Teen*, and the *Los Angeles Times* were among the high profile publications that ran interviews. *Teen* featured the Girls in a fashion spread, complete with commentary, and treated them much the way the English papers had—as new heroines for girls, which was exactly the way the Spices wanted to be seen.

America, and the whole Spice trip, had left Mel C more or less speechless—a rarity for one of the Girls. "I feel like I'm living my dream," she said, "because I can travel the world, singing and dancing with my four best friends—this is such an adventure!"

Notably, the fashions they were photographed wearing weren't *haute couture*; the most expensive piece was Mel B's sweater by DWD, which cost $110—not thrift-store prices, mind you, but still not top of the line, and completely in keeping with the Spices' image as the girls next door, the ones who'd shop in the High Street in England, or on the funky side of the mall here in the States.

But the Girls didn't need to spend a fortune to look good, although they certainly shelled out the bucks in designer Tommy Hilfiger's New York boutique. Already a fan, Hilfiger was delighted to see them, and after they left his store, he sent them even more clothing, going so far as to offer to supervise their wardrobe in their next video, absolutely free of charge.

America had taken to the Girls, and they'd taken to America.

"We absolutely love it," Geri said. "We feel completely at home here."

But it wouldn't have been a Spicy time without a hint of scandal, some "fortune," and even more fame.

The scandal came via the vastly overreported and exaggeratedly presented streaking incident, the accounts of which quickly forgot the truth—Emma, Mel B, and Geri's naked run down an empty hotel corridor—and blew it up into an all-out dash through the

hotel lobby by every member of the band, shocking the other guests beyond belief.

And then there was the problem with the Spice adult entertainment (read: porn) channel available on a pay-per-view basis in plenty of American homes. Could the Spice Girls be confused with the Spice channel? Network president Steve Saril was all ready to complain if they were. He made plans to work with a national stripper competition to name an "official Spice [channel] girl," and there was even talk of bringing together some adult-film stars to make a video lip-synching of "Wannabe." Strange, perhaps, but the Spice Girls were becoming huge business, and everyone wanted a piece of the action.

"We're taking advantage of a certain period of time in which they have a hit," Saril told the *Los Angeles Times*. "But they may not be popular for long."

He might have known his own field, but Saril was no expert on pop music. The Girls, by the way, didn't offer any comment about the plans of channel Spice (which, amazingly, hadn't tried to buy the topless shots of Geri...).

There was big money in the Spice Girls, and more of it was just around the bend.

Pepsi, always quick to spot something hot, had singled them out as the Next Big Thing and offered to star them in a commercial. The deal was rumored to involve at least a million dollars for each Girl, although the Spices themselves found these reports hilarious. "We"—*bleep*—"wish," was Mel C's comment—saying it was actually much, much less.

The spot, filmed during February, was due to air at the end of March, over the Easter weekend. However rich it did or didn't make the Girls, it was still a major deal. Pepsi had the money to buy the top names and had certainly done so in the past. By choosing the Spices, it put the business seal of approval on the Girls. More than that, it more or less guaranteed them access to every American household during commercial breaks on both network and cable television. And that, in turn, would translate into the Spices becoming as much a part of America's daily life as they were of England's, with record sales, inevitably, shooting straight through the roof.

It was important news. It meant that in one short month the cracked nut was opening to reveal the meat. No other British band, let alone one that was all female, had achieved anything like it before. As records went, there seemed to be very few that the Spices hadn't managed to break.

About the only thing missing was an American number-one album. That would have been the cherry on top of the sundae. But it didn't seem as if it was going to happen. At least, not yet. *Spice* climbed to number six, and held there during the first week of March, before slipping one spot (as the sound track to Howard Stern's movie *Private Parts* zoomed straight to number one), only to rise back to six the following week. But *Spice* has legs. As the Spice vibe infiltrates all fifty States, who knows what might happen? They're still on their first single, which was sticking firmly to the top of the charts in the second week of March. After their April 12 *Saturday Night Live* appearance, the first showings of the Pepsi commercial, and the release of "Say You'll Be There," anything could happen. Anything at all. A year ago no one would have bet on five unknown girls doing what they did. But in the Spice world, everything is possible. And Spice America remains very much the land of opportunity for these lay-dees. After all, there's a whole generation of girls waiting to be turned on to Girl Power.

The year 1997 started off every bit as strongly as '96 had closed. Mel B once said that the Spices "set out on a mission to get exactly what we wanted," and by now they had to be getting close to accomplishing it. They'd become their own best publicists, always getting in the last word, always outrageous and daring.

They were fun, and maybe that was one of the reasons America had found them so irresistible.

Victoria said, "We want girls to be able to relate to us," and there was no doubt that they did. The Spice Girls had well and truly arrived. Everywhere.

But still nowhere more than in Britain, where the first issue of the Girls' official magazine, *Spice*, hit the stands in the last week of January (as did any number of "less official" publications). Although largely written by others, the Spices made sure they were involved by writing the answers to readers' questions in the "Spice Advice" column. Indeed, said the publisher, "'Spice Advice' was one of the ideas in the magazine that came directly from the girls. Their personalities are such that the advice is very up-front. They have strong views on most things."

And their answers showed just how committed to Girl Power they remained. When "Losing It" of Perth, Australia, wanted to know how to deal with her boyfriend, who was pressuring her to sleep with him, the reply was simple: ditch 'im. Having become role models for girls, the Spices were taking their position very seriously indeed.

Chapter Fifteen

Bringing It All Back Home

*T*oward the end of February, with America in the palms of their hands, the Spice Girls returned to Britain. They were scheduled to play a charity concert in Birmingham, to help raise money for Cash For Kids, and would be the headline act in a show that featured many top names in British pop music—Peter Andre, Louise, Gabrielle, Dodgy, 911, Kavana, and Michelle Gayle.

It was a hectic week. First, on February 21, they jetted into Dublin for the Irish music IRMA Awards, in which they'd been voted the Best International Act.

Then, just three days later, they had to get themselves ready for the Big One: the night of the BRIT Awards, held in London's Earl's Court, *the* big night for British music. Already nominated in five categories, the Girls had also been asked to open the show—a rare honor for a pop band—and they immediately accepted.

As they strode on to perform a medley of "Wannabe" and "Who Do You Think You Are?" the crowd rose to its feet to see the Spices at their exuberant, outrageous best. Mel C wore a crop top and training pants, Emma was in a short, sparkling dress (purple, of course, this being a major occasion), Victoria in a bikini top and micro-skirt. Mel B wore a tight leopardskin jump suit, its zipper pulled all the way down to her navel, revealing—flaunting—a black Wonderbra.

But it was going to be Geri's night for attracting attention.

Her costume was skimpy, to say the least, red platform boots topped by the shortest dress imaginable, with a Union Jack on its front and a peace symbol on the back. Where had it come from? Who'd made it? According to *The Mirror*, the original idea had been Geri's, and it had become reality thanks to her sister, Natalie, who ran a clothing design company named Firecracker.

The dress was sensational enough to be featured on many of the front pages the next day, but the Spices—and particularly Geri—hadn't finished making their mark for the night.

Some areas of the BRITs were judged by industry professionals, and in those the Spices lost out, admittedly to bands like Manic Street Preachers, one of Mel C's current favorites. But it was the public that got to choose Best Single (voted on by listeners to commercial radio) and Best Video (picked by viewers of *The Box*, the show that had first brought the Spices to people's attention). In both those categories, the Spice Girls walked away with the awards.

And on both the occasions they walked up to the stage to accept them, Geri managed to cause a stir. She'd changed from the Union Jack mini into to sparkling red strapless number, very elegant and carefully engineered. But not quite carefully enough. Twice, as she climbed to the stage, there was a slight accident, and the crowd got to see even more of Sexy Spice than they'd bargained for that night. Using her hands for extra support, she laughed it off, saying, "If you wear a tight dress like this, you've got to expect it, and everyone's seen them before, so I don't give a damn."

She was over the top, she was a little rude, but still nice and lovable, she was...just Geri. Perhaps the real saving grace was that the show wasn't being aired live, allowing for some judicious editing before transmission.

At a post-award-show press conference, the incident of the falling dress wasn't mentioned, but the Girls were more than happy to show their appreciation for the awards. "We feel fantastic," Victoria said. "Things just seem to get better and better. Last year we came to the BRITs as guests. We were nobodies then."

Certainly they couldn't be called that anymore. And Geri was in full agreement. "We owe all our success to Britain," she announced.

The reporters were also eager to know how the Spices had reacted to their recent American success. By now, combined U.S. sales of "Wannabe" and *Spice* had topped a million copies.

"We're just proud to be ambassadors of pop for our country," Geri answered. "Everyone, especially us, has been amazed at how fast we've hit America. We've done it faster than The Beatles."

But there was no danger of them moving across the Atlantic to settle in the L.A. sun or get caught up in the New York bustle. A couple of weeks earlier, *The Sun* had published a story that claimed the Girls would soon be making their homes in the U.S. "While they love England," it concluded, "they know if they have success in America, they must move."

Mel C's mother, Joan, had already gone some way to scotching that rumor when she said, "There's no way they'll go. All the girls are far too close to their families."

But now they had the chance to dispel the rumors for themselves, and they did it in no uncertain manner. "We'd never do it," Geri said firmly. "We love Britain too much and we're proud to be British."

The BRIT Awards show was a huge moment for the Spices, a chance to get some recognition for their

hard-won triumph. And they made the most of the evening. "We had a brilliant time and were behaving like fans," Geri said. "We kept seeing all these famous people. Diana Ross came up to us and we had to have our photo taken with her. She is a legend."

While it was a night for champagne and celebration for the Spices (and for a look-alike band called A Touch of Spice, who succeeded in crashing the ceremony), one person did try to wreck the joy they must have felt. Liam Gallagher, the surly lead singer of Oasis, had publicly declared that he wouldn't be attending the awards show because he would "probably chin"—i.e., punch—"the Spice Girls."

Those were fighting words from a man with a temper. The previous year Gallagher had managed to insult both the presenter of an award and another guest. But the Spices, always feisty and never shy, weren't about to stand for any abuse. And they weren't about to let their night be ruined, issuing a challenge from the stage.

"I'd just like to see him try," Mel B said. "I'd quite enjoy getting in a fight with him. Come on, Liam, I dare you. Show us just how tough you are."

Of course, no one would have expected anything less from them. And Emma managed the final sting when she said, "We all much prefer [Liam's brother] Noel, anyway. He's really nice and he's the talented one."

News of the argument obviously reached Noel Gallagher, and later in the evening he apologized to the Girls for his brother's rude remarks.

The awards done, it was time for the Girls to look ahead. Incredible achievements aside, there was still plenty of work to do.

Some had wondered why they'd chosen to perform "Who Do You Think You Are?" at the BRITs, and there was a good reason for the decision. The Spices had become involved with British Comic Relief and an event to raise money for the homeless called Red Nose Day, to be held on March 14. They'd signed on to be spokespeople for the event, and soon pictures were appearing of them in Comic Relief T-shirts and big red clown noses to help publicize the day.

Now, it just so happened that "Who Do You Think You Are?" was the theme song for Comic Relief '97, and was due for release as a single early in March, with all the profits going to the charity—a sum estimated at half a million pounds sterling. It was a sweet gesture, even if the Girls could well afford to make it these days. But they were pleased to be a part of it all. "We're thrilled to be involved," Emma announced. "Comic Relief is a great fun day with a brilliant cause."

Even the video for the song had a comic angle, featuring the Spices and a specially put together group of celebrity "look-alikes," known as the Sugar Lumps.

There was British TV star Jennifer Saunders as Geri, her stage partner Dawn French as Victoria, along with singer Lulu posing as Emma, and Kathy Burke and Llewella Gideon.

"I was absolutely dumbfounded," Geri said later. "Jennifer looked exactly like me. I just shrieked...then I burst out laughing."

While they were filming the video, in February, news came throught that "Wannabe" had reached the top of the American charts. It should have been cause for a massive celebration, but there just wasn't the time.

"We went mad, jumping up and down and screaming," Geri recalled. "It was a fantastic moment none of us will ever forget. Then the director shouted 'action,' and we went back to work."

With the Spices back from America and on full public view at the BRITs, the reporters were back at work, digging up whatever new gossip they could find on the Girls. And it seemed there was plenty.

Since her return, Geri had acquired a phone stalker, according to the *Daily Express*. Around the end of February, she received a number of anonymous, obscene calls, all from the same person. With the help of British Telecom's tracing system, she was able to find his number, and even considered calling in the police. But according to a friend, "after talking it over with the other four girls in the group," she "decided it was better to find out who it was before she made any complaint," and so she hired a private detective.

But all scandal mongering was left in the dust by the news the Girls received at the beginning of March. Their new single, "Mama," released as a double A-side with "Who Do You Think You Are?," had appeared on the third of the month, going straight in at number one, with advance orders for 600,000 copies. This put the Spices into the history books. *No* other band's first four singles had reached number one. In fact, only one other group, Take That, had ever managed four consecutive number ones.

The timing was perfect, with Comic Relief coming up, and Mother's Day in Britain being celebrated on March 9. Even so, said Mel C, "It is absolutely incredible."

The video for "Mama," like the Comic Relief clip, had been filmed in February. An old warehouse was transformed for the shoot into a fake television studio broadcasting *Spice TV* (absolutely no relation to its racy American cable counterpart), filled with children and their parents, all part of a "studio audience" for a game show featuring not only the Spices, but also—indeed, especially—their mums.

It was meant to be a thank-you to their mothers, and that was exactly how it turned out. All the Spice mums were involved, and Mel B made sure Andrea Brown had a wonderful time. "She really enjoyed it," Mel said later, "and it was great for her to see what we do for a living."

Spicemania had heated up again, all the way to boiling, and now even the government was getting in on the act. In the House of Commons, no less a personage than the chancellor of the exchequer quoted from "Wannabe," while other Conservative members of Parliament urged ministers to congratulate the Girls for not becoming tax exiles, for winning the BRIT Awards, and most of all, for their claim that Margaret Thatcher was the original Spice Girl.

Had it all gotten completely out of hand?

Perhaps, but it's not about to stop now. The ball is rolling and it's not going to slow down. The rest of the Spices' year is already mapped out in minute detail.

They've already recorded their next single, a cover of "5-4-3-2-1," which was a British smash for Manfred Mann more than three decades ago. While it's planned as the theme song for the new British television network, Channel 5, it might end up as the follow-up to "Mama."

Summer will see them filming their movie, in Los Angeles, possibly with veteran Dick Lester—the man who directed both *A Hard Day's Night* and *Help!* for The Beatles—behind the camera.

No sooner will that be finished than they'll have to start writing songs for their second album, which will be recorded in the fall. As if that's not enough on their plates, "We've got a big one-off [one-time only] show in Britain planned for October," Geri revealed in *The Sun*. Although she wouldn't specify the location, it will almost certainly be the Wembley Arena, the only place large enough to hold the legions of their fans. But the biggest surprise of all was yet to come, when Geri announced, "We're going to do a world tour. It will start in February [1998]."

It's tough to reach the top, but life obviously doesn't get any easier once you've arrived. The Spices are proof of that. Having succeeded, the pressure becomes stronger than ever to keep succeeding. They have no time to themselves.

For the moment, though, they don't mind. They can take it all in stride. They have the energy and the vitality to see themselves through the grueling hours of work. Having come so far, it's difficult to forget that they're still a very new phenomenon. Less than a year ago nobody had heard of them.

Once they're fully established, with a substantial body of work behind them, they'll be able to settle down a little, to relax. The pressure will ease. For now, though, being a pop band means that they constantly have to keep proving themsleves.

But no precedent exists for a singing team like the Spice Girls, no previous group they can model themselves on. They're blazing a trail, not only for themselves, but for all the girls who will undoubtedly follow them.

They're everywhere, in everything. There's even talk of a Spicy CD-ROM, tentatively called *Five Go Mad in Cyberspace*, which would give them a place even on the frontiers of technology.

So what can the future really hold for the Spices? Love and marriage, probably, but those events won't break up the group. They've been through so much together already, and the bonds are so strong, as is their sense that friends have to stick together. How far can they take this success? The road ahead seems to stretch to infinity. Magazines, films, television...and, of course, music—there's no area where they can't make their mark, and along the way influence a whole new female generation. They've even conquered the Internet, as Web sites dedicated to the Fab Five spring up every day.

Could it all die down as quickly as it's blown up? That seems doubtful. The Girls have such a groundswell of support, support that only continues to grow all the time, that it would be impossible for them simply to disappear from the scene. In all likelihood, during the next five years the Girls will experience some remarkable growth both artistically and personally. While they've made the kind of start that has them labeled as a pop phenomenon, given time, their vision of what they really, really want will probably get clearer, and they'll have the means to achieve their desires. What that vision might be remains to be seen—it's doubtful that they even know themselves yet. Then they'll *truly* be the voice of a generation.

But it'll always involve a lot of fun. It would be impossible to think of Geri, Mel B, Mel C, Victoria, and Emma having anything else. For a supposedly manufactured group they've broken out of any mold that could have cramped and deformed them, gone their own way, and become an even bigger sensation because of it. They've shown that nothing in the world is strong enough to stifle Girl Power, and that you can realize your heart's strongest desire.

Above all else, they've shown us what it means to *zigzig-ha*. They've given us everything, and they won't stop for a long, long time.

A Spicy Timeline

August 8, 1972	Geraldine Estelle Halliwell born.
January 12, 1974	Melanie Jayne Chisholm born.
April 7, 1975	Victoria Addams born.
May 29, 1975	Melanie Janine Brown born.
January 21, 1976	Emma Lee Bunton born.
March 1994	Four hundred girls answer an ad in *The Stage*. Geri, Mel B, Mel C, Victoria, and Michelle Stephenson are picked to form a group called Touch.
May 1994	Michelle leaves. Abigail Kis auditions, doesn't join. Emma Bunton is selected as a replacement.
May 1995	The Spice Girls sign with manager Simon Fuller.
July 1995	They win a recording contract with Virgin Records.
Fall 1995	The Spice Girls write and record their songs.
March 1996	The "Wannabe" video airs on *The Box*.
April/May 1996	The Girls tour radio stations and seaside resorts.
June 24, 1996	"Wannabe" is released.
July 27, 1996	"Wannabe" hits number one in England, and stays there for seven weeks, while going to the top in thirty other countries.

September 23, 1996	"Say You'll Be There" released and enters the chart at number one, to stay there for two weeks.
November 1996	*Spice* released. Enters the British album charts at number one. The Spice Girls turn on London's Christmas lights.
December 1996	"2 Become 1" released and enters the chart at number one. The Spice Girls have the top Christmas single in Britain.
January 1997	The Spices begin a publicity tour of America. "Wannabe" is released in the U.S. and enters the chart at number eleven.
February 1997	*Spice* is released in America, entering the album chart at number six. "Wannabe" climbs to number one.
February 24, 1997	The Spice Girls win two BRIT Awards.
March 3, 1997	"Mama"/"Who Do You Think You Are?" is issued in Britain and enters the chart at number one, giving the Girls a historic fourth straight top hit with their first four singles.
March 14, 1997	The Spice Girls celebrate Red Nose Day by supporting British Comic Relief.
March 22, 1997	After three weeks atop the *Billboard* Hot 100, "Wannabe" slips from number one.
April 12, 1997	The Spice Girls appear on *Saturday Night Live*.

FINDING SOME SPICE

Getting in touch with the Spice Girls isn't difficult. In the United States, they can be reached at:

Girl Power

P.O. Box 8863

Red Bank, NJ 07701

If you have access to a computer, there are now literally thousands of Spice sites on the World Wide Web. A great links page is at **http://www.users.dircon.co.uk/~ecs/ The_Spice_Girls/links.html,** which also has a Spicy Search engine.

But to start you off, here are some of the better sites around. Virgin, naturally, has the official Spice Girls site. If you go there, be sure to take the time to check out the Girls' pencil case:

http://channel3.vmg.co.uk/spicegirls/

The other sites are all unofficial, but that doesn't mean they're not good. All of the following contain plenty of pictures and information. Some have great audio and video clips as well:

Spice Ring: **http://shaw.iol.ie/~kasst//spice/ring.htm**

Spicegirls.com: **http://www.spicegirls.com/**

Say You'll Be There: **http://www.geocities.com/ SunsetStrip/Alley/7425/**

Spice Shack: **http://web.online.co.uk/Members/ gary.fenton/**

Emma's Spicy Page: **http://www.angelfire.com/co/fitn-funky/spicegirls.html**

David's Page: **http://www.wantree.com.au/~biggs/
spicegirls/index.html**

Virtual Spice: **http://ireland.iol.ie/~kasst/spice/**

U.K. fan club: **http://www.xs4all.nl/`tob/fancl_uk.htm**

Spice Online: **http://biodec.wustl.edu/matt/spice/**

German Page: **http://members.sol.com/spicegirlz/
index.htm**

Swedish fan club: **http://homepage.calypso.net/~ci10151/
spicegirls.html**

Dutch fan club: **http://www.xs4all.nl/~tob**

Super Spice Girls Page: **http://www.jrfsm.demon.co.uk/
spice_girls/index.htm**

And, of course, there are more appearing every day.

You can also subscribe to the Spice Girls mailing list by sending an E-mail to Majordomo@spicegirls.com with the word *subscribe* in the body of the message.

ACKNOWLEDGMENTS

As with any book, many more people than the writer are involved. I'm merely one cog in the machine. And so I have to thank my amazing agent, Madeleine Morel, for opportunities and trust. My editor, Maureen O'Neal, and her staff have been wonderful to work with.

And then there are Toby and Jamie, the incredible Spice Boys. Not forgetting Greg, either. Dave, of course, for the hint. My mum and dad, to whom I owe all of this, really. The remarkable Peter Trowell in London, who always seems to come up trumps. The woman on the West Coast who needs to remain anonymous— thank you. And, as always, Linda and Graham, for love and patience. Where would I be without the two of you?

A number of articles proved invaluable in my research for this book: "Spice Girls" by Chris Heath, *The Face,* March 1997; "1997: A Spice Odyssey" by Damon Syson, *Sky International*, February 1997; "Biscuit Tin," *Smash Hits*, January 29, 1997; "Revealed: How the Spice Girls Couldn't Sing a Note," by Ceri Jackson and Annabel Cole, *Daily Mail*, February 1997; "The Spice Girls," by Jancee Dunn, *Rolling Stone*, March 6, 1997; "Spice Girls," *DJ Times*, February 1997; "Manufactured in Britain. Now Selling in America," by Steve Pond, *The New York Times*, February 16, 1997; "Spice Like Us," by Robyn Forest, *Bikini*, March 1997; "Spice and Everything Catchy," by Jerry Crowe, *Los Angeles Times*, February 8, 1997; "Taking On the Britpop Boys," by Paul Gorman, *Music Week*, April 1996; "Girls On Top," by Mike Flaherty, *Entertainment Weekly*, February 21–28, 1997; "We're Brits with Hits," by Andy